...and the little girl cries.

Written by Wapani Savage

Acknowledgments

I am honored to have the aide and expertise from a handful of people in putting this book together. I would like to thank Julia Morton for taking my thoughts for a cover and creating a beautiful piece of art, and for laying out and formatting my book. She did a wonderful job.

I thank my mom, Voncele Savage, for her patience during my moments of epiphany or despair; either way, she listens to me. Thank you.

Ty Emmecca, my brother, your guidance and words of wisdom helped me to learn how to utilize every aspect of the cosmos for self-healing, as well as teaching me how to reach out to others.

Introduction

...My father was enraged by my unyielding posture. Like a savaged beast, he ripped the covers out of my hands and away from the bed in one quick sweep, totally exposing my trembling body. A whirlwind was growing in intensity as he grabbed my legs and wrenched them apart. I heard roaring in my ears escalating into a crescendo. He was on top of me, crushing my breath away. Demon eyes, breath heated from hell on my face. Then – blank.

This horrific scene is not from a fictitious book, nor any horror movie. It is a part of my childhood. Moments like this one forged the foundation of my life, compelling me to reach out to other women who have experienced the same type of terror and devastation. It is my desire for others to know that they are not alone. Women have silently dealt with their shame from sexual abuse. Those feelings have gone on unquestioned and not discussed. So many little girls have been molested, our flower taken from us and tainted at such an incredibly young age. Molestation has taken place in the lives of nearly 33% of girls before the age of 18, according to The US Justice Department. These are just the *recorded* cases. Many women never tell anyone about the abuse for fear of retaliation or degradation. The very subject is taboo, hence adults are reluctant to broach the subject with their daughters. Those hurting girls grow up to be bitter and distant women, yearning for healing and no salve to be found for their wound.

While I knew that other women had been violated as children, I felt powerless to do anything about it. So many questions and doubts constantly swirled within my mind that it snatched my sleep at night and my concentration during the day. How does one reach out to other hurting people if their own wounds had not healed? I continued asking myself the infinitesimal question, *why me*, while wondering, *why did I suffer the way I did*? Why am I still dealing with the emotional aftershocks from quakes that happened long ago? Is there a God and does that Divine Being care about me?

The past is where I began searching for the answers. I have since learned that the roots of the present are deeply anchored within the past. Because my past is full of lies and deception, my quest was fueled by a deep need for truth, uncompromised. I felt compelled to study spiritual texts beyond the scope of Christianity, as well as science and eventually quantum physics. Out of those journals and reams of notes came the birthing of this book. I truly believe that the knowledge and understanding gained while writing has been the best counseling I have ever received. Hopefully, if you are reading this book, you will receive that needed healing and emotional transformation, as well.

1

As a little girl, I was an extrovert. I smiled abundantly, talked endlessly and touched everyone and everything. Loving everyone and finding great joy in living, it did not matter if I had just met someone or had known him or her my whole life. I would hug and kiss them, telling everyone I loved them. I truly believed all people were beautiful. The way people responded to me was the exact same way I looked upon others.

My childhood appeared to be no different then any one else's. My parents bought their first house when I was three. It was a two-story brick house with a big yard and a dog. The elementary school was right across the street. After school, kids would race home to change clothes. Five minutes later, you would see boys riding their bicycles or skateboards up and down the streets. Little ladies played jacks, hopscotch or double-dutch on the sidewalks. Our neighborhood was considered safe and was bustling with new families getting a fresh start in life.

After we had lived there for about two years, a neighbor had a 'block warming' party welcoming all new families to the community. As we walked into their backyard that day, I was awestruck by the different people. Racing past me was a vivacious little girl with four braids – or plats, as we called them - in her hair. Each plat pursued its own direction. She wore bib overalls without a shirt and was running circles around the yard, the house, anything that was stationary, screaming at the top of her lungs just for the sake of hollering. She was a unique cross-eyed child. Everything about her was in utter contrast from me. She was carefree and jovial while I maintained, until it felt okay for me to run my mouth, and that I did, often. There was also another little girl there. She was shy and quiet, clinging to her mother. The three of us were as diverse as a plantain from a mango or kiwi. Tessie was six years old, spirited, and a born leader. Monica was four years old, subtle, sweet and timid. I was five years old, talkative and observant. We became inseparable.

My brother and I were raised to be on our best behavior at all times or –as my mom would put it – be on our 'ps' and 'qs'. Mom was not bitter or harsh with me. She possessed an authority that did not need to be sonorous. Just a certain look cast my was enough – most of the time. During weekdays, our activities were mostly limited to the home. However, on Saturdays, mom had errands to run which meant a day of being out and about. It did not matter if it was just a trip to the mall - and there were several in Prince Georges County, Maryland - or just going to the drycleaners and grocery store. If we were well behaved, the day would end with a treat. When we would go to Iverson mall, mom would stop by the Baskin Robins ice cream parlor. She would allow us to pick our favorite flavor. Mine was butter brickle. My mom would always have to start my cone. If she did not, only half of the ice cream would make it into my mouth. The other half would end up on my face and hands or down the front of my clothes.

Good behavior was a given at my house. I do not remember my parents yelling much when I was a young child. It was more of an expression they would give us. If that 'look' from my mom was not enough, she had a three-strikes-and-you're-out method of discipline. The first strike would be a direct order.

You kids stop all of that noise.

The second strike would be reinforcement and a warning.

Didn't I tell you two to quiet down?! Don't make me come up there!

The third strike would be a very persuasive whuppin'.

We had a very short, stringent list of unspoken rules in our house. We seemed to be born knowing not to challenge them.

1. Never say no.
2. Never ask why.
3. Do as you were told. Period.

My friends would refer to my parents as strict. Our household rules were steady and consistent when I was a child. Our mom would wake us every morning at 7:30, no matter what the season. We were expected to clean our bedrooms meticulously every morning or we did not eat breakfast. This particular rule never had to be enforced. I tell you what; I would rather get a whuppin' than to have to endure my mom's mouth! She had a knack, as most moms do, for going on and on and on about which infraction we would make.

I know you don't think this room is clean. You have toys under the bed. Where do they belong? Your bed isn't made; your doll doesn't belong there. What have I told you about throwing your clothes on the floor? Do you think that I tell you to do something just to hear myself talk? Girl, you've lost your mind. Put those skates up...

Almost every morning, we had a hot breakfast. Even if we had a bowl of cereal, we would have hot toast with apple butter, as well. My mom was home during the summer; therefore, our daily activities were usually mapped out. Each day always ended with my brother and I on the couch, cuddled on either side of her as she read to us. She was great at becoming each character in the story, giving me the feeling of actually being there. I could almost hear that panther talking or those waves smashing against the breakers. I could almost smell that ham frying as she wrinkled her nose at the thought of consuming green eggs. After our story, we were in bed by seven thirty.

I began to learn independence at the ripe old age of five. My parents owning a beautiful home did not mean that they were wealthy. A baby sitter was a luxury they could not afford. My mother would place a lunch tray in the guest bedroom with a sandwich, a piece or two of fruit, and a glass of milk. There was a small 13" black and white TV in there and mom would give me a quick lesson in the do's and don'ts.

Now, baby, your dad and I have to go to work. Stay in this room. Don't come out unless you have to use the bathroom. Your lunch is right here. Behave yourself, you hear me?

I knew better than to disobey my mom. I stayed in that room. While in there, I found solace within the land of fantasy. I became any character shown on TV. I would become a jeanie one moment, a giant robot the next. I was not a pillar of courage. Fear was a constant companion, be it a fear of bees, spiders, the boogieman, dogs, or thunderstorms. By keeping the bedroom door closed, I controlled my fears of the boogieman. To me, that door was the only barrier stopping the monsters from getting me. I would devour my lunch before ten o'clock, overcome with hunger and relief when I heard keys rattling at the front door at the end of each day.

I was also terribly afraid of the dark. It was a tangible entity to me: alive, breathing, evil. It watched me, waiting for the right moment to close in and eat me, especially at bedtime. The covers would be pulled over my head with just enough room for a little fresh air gap. That is where I put the covers and that is where they stayed until morning. I figured if I could not see the monsters, then they would not get me because I did not provoke them by looking at them.

One other respite against my fears was music. My room and my brother's room were on the top floor. There was only a two and a half year difference between our ages, Tyrone being the oldest. We would lie in our beds with the door, dividing the two rooms, open. We would sing until one voice or the other trailed off into slumber. The one left awake would respect that and continue to hum quietly until they too fell asleep. We were able to keep the beat by lying on our stomachs, wrapping our arms around our pillows and bopping our heads up and down to the rhythm of each song. We had never seen each other partake in this practice, yet it was still a shared habit.

Our bedtime custom was born from an environment rich with culture and music. My mom was a music teacher. She exposed us to many diverse cultures through music. If her class were going on a field trip, she would pull us from our classes at our schools and take us with her. We have been to operas, symphonies, ballet, and other forms of musical expression. Later, music became a lifeline between my sanity and me.

2

I started kindergarten when I was six. I was placed in the afternoon sessions. Mom was comfortable allowing one of the neighbors to care for me until twelve thirty. She lived a few houses down from ours. When I got there in the mornings, I would plant myself in front of the TV to watch the cartoons. Our parents would not allow us to watch most of what came on TV, let alone choose what we wanted to watch; therefore, when I went to other peoples' homes, it received my full attention. Every morning, the babysitter, Mrs. Wallace, had to get on my case about sitting so close to the TV. I would sit close enough to feel the hair-raising, prickly electricity coming from the screen. We found out later that I was extremely near sighted and needed glasses.

Sometimes Mrs. Wallace and I would ride over to

a school where she knew one of the staff members who worked in the cafeteria. The three of us would have a seat perched upon stools at the serving counter. The two adults would casually chat while sipping coffee. Mrs. Wallace poured me half of a cup, not without much skepticism from her friend.

Girl, does her momma let her drink coffee?

Aw, that little bit ain't gonna hurt her.

That staff member then turned to me, a knowing twinkle in her eye.

Baby, do you understand that this is a grown-up's drink? You must be awfully big to drink coffee,

To which Mrs. Wallace replied,

April's a big girl. She can handle this little bit and keep her mouth shut about it.

Let me tell you, I was feeling like an adult at that moment! I did not want to come across like a kid, so I just kept my mouth shut, drank the pungent coffee and put on the most grown-up face and posture that a six-year-old girl could muster. As long as I lived there on Nova Ave., I never told anyone that Mrs. Wallace allowed me to drink coffee.

I enjoyed going to the Wallace's house. Mrs. Wallace had two sons and a daughter. Michael was Tyrone's age and the other son was a relatively young teenager. One Saturday, I was bored. I assumed my mom grew tired of me being underfoot. She said that I could go to Mrs. Wallace's house with my brother. Once we arrived at their house, Tyrone and Michael decided to play hide and seek. They went to hide, I was *it* and the older son was supposed to stay with me to make sure I did not peek. His idea of restraint was not conventional.

Shhh. Stay quiet and lie down. I can't let you see where they're going.

He then covered my body with his own. I felt his maleness becoming hard against me. Not understanding what was happening, I just grimaced, sucking air in through my clinched teeth. He was hurting me. He immediately got up, a faint smirk and a glint of mischief in his eyes.

Don't tell anybody. You'll get in trouble.

He then went on with the game as though nothing had happened. As a child, I did not analyze the incident, even though it became imprinted upon my mind. The only emotions felt were confusion and fear. I could not comprehend why someone would do that to me. A child seems to remain carefree as long as their experiences remain positive. Introducing negative energy into one's life causes mental and emotional barriers to be erected around that person's heart. It is human nature to respond to danger by protecting ourselves in an attempt to deflect any future arrows of suffering.

My mind responded by creating fictitious scenario's of what I would do if I were in that position again. My dream patterns changed, as kaos was introduced into my thought stream. I did not consciously dwell on what had happened, even though the experience burrowed itself deep into my subconscious. There were many experiences that added to the foundation of my subconscious.

The previous summer, before kindergarten, my mom enrolled me into summer camp at a neighboring school. Camp involved arts and crafts, nature hikes through the woods, snacks, and swimming. Free-play was scheduled at the end of the day. This allowed the children to either stay and play or just go home. The school had a community pool. Even though I did not know how to swim, and was too afraid to learn, I still enjoyed getting into the water at the shallow end.

Our neighborhood consisted of at least ten or more blocks. Children living on the blocks surrounding mine attended the school across the street from my house. The children living on the blocks further down Nova Ave. attended the neighboring school. At camp, I met a 7-year-old little boy who attended that neighboring school. His name was Chris. During free-play, he would give me a shove, sending me careening down the sliding board. In the pool, he would generally play with the boys (of course), but every now and then, he would doggy paddle over to the shallow end and splash water in my face, always making a hasty retreat before I could retaliate.

On the last day of camp, during free-play, Chris came over to where I played on the merry-go-round and asked me to follow him. I was suspicious, even though I was only six. He saw my hesitance, flashed a playful smile and said,

Aw, come on,

As he gently took my hand, giving it a subtle tug, my hesitation dissolved as I allowed myself to be led toward the opposite side of the school.

No one was on that side of the school. Chris slowed his stroll and began peaking into the windows, looking into each room as we worked our way further away from the people and sounds of camp. He gestured for me to come quickly to a particular window, stating proudly that it was his classroom. I came up closely so that the both of us could cup our hands around our eyes, pressing our faces against the window to peer inside. His attention left his classroom, coming to rest fully upon my face. As I returned his gaze, he quickly closed the gap between us and planted a kiss squarely on my lips. He lingered only for a second or two then stepped back a pace, searching my face intently for any sign of approval. The only message he should have been able to read was one of surprise. I thought, *why did you do that, and what are we supposed to do now?*

He then told me to follow him as he started across the short expanse of grass separating the school from the row of houses that lined the street. We ended up on the porch of an abandoned house. As we sat down, Indian style, he said,

Let's play like we're married.

I shrugged an, *okay*. He then kissed me again. After several childlike, fumbly kisses, I told him that I needed to be heading home. Without a word, he picked himself up and headed back toward the school, stopping only to look over his shoulder for a fleeting glance. He briefly flashed that smile, and then resumed his course, using a boyish gallop all the way back around the corner of the school. I also got up from the porch, but instead of going back and playing at the school, I walked the three blocks home, thinking about Chris' kisses.

3

I idolized my father. I used to hang on his every word. I quietly observed him with the awe and admiration that every little girl shows and feels for her daddy. I felt a surge of love and anticipation every evening when mom announced that daddy was home. My mom would head to the front door and I, being close on her heels, would meet my dad as he climbed the front steps. With his briefcase in one hand, keys and hat in the other, dad would reach to open the door just as mom swung it open, lovingly planting a kiss on his lips. I would wait my turn, feeling special when dad looked at me, giving his 'sweetheart', (that is what he called me) her affection and kisses as well.

In the mornings, I would rush to finish my preparations for school, timing my completion just right so that I could take my post in the bathroom doorway and watch my dad shave his face. I enjoyed questioning him endlessly while I watched in fascination as he smoothed on Blue Magic shaving cream. I liked the peculiar eggy smell it held. I would lean against that door jam, looking up into the mirror watching his reflection as intently as he did, while making sure to place the cream precisely where it needed to go. I returned five minutes later to observe him using his designated butter knife, carefully scraping the hardened cream from his face. It was like magic to me. One moment he had stubble. After smoothing the weird cream onto his face and waiting for five minutes, suddenly his face was smooth. Of course, I had to try out his freshly shaven cheeks to make sure it worked.

My dad did not lavish his children with idle words purporting love, nor did he show us his love through physical means. He tried to spread a little sunshine the best way he knew how - road trips. Those were the times of peace and complete happiness in my house. It would either consist of a simple one day outing to the ocean or to the mountains. We also had those one or two weeklong planned vacations. When it was a simple one-day ride, mom awoke us early, gently whispering,

Come on. Get yourselves together. We're going riding.

The magic words! Sometimes, we went to Ocean City a couple of hours away. We would stop for hand-dipped ice cream at *High's* convenience store. As usual, mom needed to start my cone. Other times, we would go view the mountains of Sky Line Drive, with its deep valleys and spring water jetting out from the rocks on the side of the mountain. My favorite vacations, however, were the planned ones. They were extended expanses of carefree abandon.

The anticipation would begin building about a week before our departure with the magic springing forth from the lowest level in our house. Our basement consisted of a utility room, a half bathroom, a laundry room and a large family room with a bar. Behind the bar were shelves where dad kept his musical equipment. He would sit down there behind the bar and compile his favorite music, which consisted mostly of blues and jazz, onto 8-tracks when I was small, and cassettes when I was older. These compilations would be our traveling music. His being behind the bar would set the stage for lighthearted anticipation.

My brother and I would lie on our stomachs on the carpet and play *SORRY* or some other board game. Mom sat on a stool at the bar sipping *ginger ale* (that's what we were told), smiling contently, watching my dad bop his head to whatever tune he was playing. Sometimes, I would get the added treat of getting to be in dads' sanctuary behind the bar. I would sit back there upon my own stool with a glass of real ginger ale feeling very special while flipping through dads various record covers. We drank only water, milk or orange juice. Having the ginger ale was outside of the rules.

The night before leaving, my brother and I would hop and bounce around the living room tickling each other chanting,

I'm so excited! I'm so excited!

My mom would pack our luggage and prepare sandwiches and a thermos full of orange juice. We would try to stay awake as long as possible just because we were allowed to do so. Early the next morning, usually around three or four o'clock, my dad would wake up, ready to go. His reasoning behind our leaving at this ungodly hour was to miss the rush hour traffic. Mom would make sure we had everything, including blankets and pillows. She would turn on the timers for the lights in the house, we'd all pile into the car, my brother and I making sure we were positioned behind our own personally designated parent. Because we did not control many aspects of our childhood, we began to pattern our own actions, ever embracing more rules for ourselves; limits.

I was mostly excited about the fact that we seemed to be breaking all of our rules. We were supposed to be in bed well before three o'clock in the morning, yet here we were, pulling away, leaving behind sleeping friends and neighbors. For an entire week or two, we would stay up later than seven thirty. We would watch TV and view something besides what was usually allowed. We would eat more of the food that we, as children, like to eat. With everything and everyone ready, off we would go under the cloak of darkness.

Breaking through the mountains of Virginia, it was a though we had gone thru a metamorphosis as we meandered closer to Mississippi. No more mountains, just flatlands. The climate differed as well. Even though Maryland is humid during the summer months, the south is more humid. As we drove along, I noticed heat waves wafting along the pavement, and grain silos, complete with cows and horses, marking the fields in the background. I observed fewer homes but with larger land area surrounding those homes. In Maryland, we had just about every insect that Mississippi had only on a smaller more timid scale. In my eyes, I truly believed the mosquitoes in Mississippi were large and abundant enough to carry a person away. The mosquitoes and stifling heat seemed to be the only downfalls of those visits.

Every year, we went to Mississippi for my dad's family reunion, which was traditionally scheduled to take place on the 4th of July. After 12 or so hours, I began to see familiar landmarks. Louise was very *small town*. There were approximately twelve or so houses on the dead-end street where we would visit with our family. Of those houses, dads' kin-folk occupied probably eight or nine. We would pull the car onto the empty lot between my cousin and her neighbor's home. Every dog sent out an alarm alerting the locals that strangers were approaching, gaining the desired affect. Relatives would peak through curtains, everyone wanting to know who owned the shiny black Cadillac El Dorado. My father had a sister who also went to the family reunion. She, along with her husband, her daughter and her niece, would make a later entrance in a luxury car of their own, always coming with a new wardrobe and displaying the perfect image of prosperity.

During our week of festivities, there was much fun to be had by a kid. Back in the '70's, we did not have video games nor did we possess any expensive toys. None of the children piled into someone's home to watch TV. My mom referred to it as the *boob tube*. We actually had fun without down loading our brains into the television or without ever spending a dime. We would play double-dutch using old clotheslines as the jump ropes, or we would play kick the can or spin the bottle, darting rocks at the bottle to send it endlessly rotating. My feet would become acclimated to walking barefoot along the gravel roads.

One of the highlights of my visits before he passed away was my Uncle Nepher's – better known as Uncle Nee's – candy store. Uncle Nee was blind; therefore, he memorized the room within his home from which he sold the candy. Each item had its own designation on any particular shelf, and he knew where every popsicle, soda pop, candy bar and lollipop was positioned. The children would come running to his window and he would be there selling his candy, potato chips, and pops, charging far less money then any store. Once, I went inside and offered to help him tidy up the little room. I swept his floor but he did not allow me to touch anything else for fear of my moving something out of order, which would disrupt his system. After I had finished, he surprised me by compensating my efforts with a bottle of Coca-Cola. It made me feel special and valued.

I believe Mississippi has some of the best cooks in the country. You haven't had good cookin' until you've had southern cookin'. I counted the days until Independence Day. The men would take large metal trash barrels, cut them in half along the length of them. Then they would screw hinges onto them, reattaching the two halves. These would become our bbq pits. The morning of Independence Day, we would wake up to the tantalizing smells of ham hocks boiling for greens, and potatoes and eggs boiling for potato salad. Pork ribs, chicken portions, beefsteaks, pork butts, everything that was barbequeable was placed on the grill early in the morning so that they would be fully cooked by noon or *dinner* as it was referred to in the south. The evening meal was called supper.

Mommas would be ready to smack a hand away from trying to pilfer a hot dog from the grill. Dads would set up the music on screened-in front porches, preparing the atmosphere. By dinnertime, we heard blues bands up and down the street as people gathered around various bbq pits to fill their plates. Collard greens, cold slaw, potato salad, chitterlings, bbq, corn bread, homemade sweet potato pie, you name it. My food would finally digest just in time for supper when I would start all over again.

4

I enjoyed going to Mississippi about as much as I enjoyed visiting Illinois, Missouri, Ohio, Indiana, California or any of the various states we have been blessed to experience. One of my father's desires for the enrichment of his children was for us to travel through every state in our country. By the time I was a teenager, we had gone to or through just about every state as well as Canada.

Even though both parents made it a priority to raise bright, well-educated, independent children, I started sensing more so then actually viewing a slow, powerful erosion. I remember as far back as the age of three and I recall a father full of fun, spontaneity, wisdom, patience and a logic that usually went far beyond the comprehension of the highest educated minds. Unfortunately, my father began showing a side of his personality that I was unaccustomed to seeing. It started out as small occasional criticisms, usually concerning the quality of our grades or the substance of any particular meal that had been prepared by my mom. If we brought home a 'B', it could have been an 'A'. If we brought home an 'A', how come it was not an 'A+'. If an 'A+', why had we not done the extra credit.

My mom would get up early in the morning to prepare a hot breakfast for her family. You name it and she would attempt to make it, be it homemade biscuits, sausage, or pancakes; what ever my father required. My father would descend into the kitchen and take one look at whatever my mom had painstakingly made. He would carry those pots and pans into the dining room, tossing them all out the backdoor.

This food isn't even fit for the dog to eat. Your mother didn't bother to teach you how to cook? Not that you're able to learn how to do anything right anyway.

Mom would stand there dejected, her head bowed, preparing more food for my brother and I while my father grabbed his car keys and left the house, slamming the front door so hard that the house seemed to shake. The sound of it and emotion behind it felt like a hammer slamming into the pit of my stomach. My father would leave Saturday morning and sometimes would not return until late Sunday night.

This was not his daily behavior when I was a small child. In the beginning, his actions were usually normal. I guess I would describe my father as being an extremist. He seemed to suffer severe mood swings. Either he was in the mood to tear down everyone around him, destroying the least bit of our pride, or he would be in the mood to show everyone a good time. A good example would be holidays. Be it Independence Day, Thanksgiving, Christmas or Halloween, holidays were celebrated to the fullest.

Halloweens were exclusively my mom's doing. She was the one to put together Halloween parties for her children or to plan anything else that went along with it. Decorative ghosts and witches were hung around the house. The largest pumpkin was brought home for my brother and me to gut and carve, creating either a smiling, happy Jack-O-Lantern or a scowling, scary looking one.

We were not allowed to go trick-or-treating. I assume my mom did not feel it was safe for her children to roam the streets after dark. We would stay home and greet the ghost, vampires, and skeletons at our front door with the miniature candy bars, bubble gum and lollipops that mom had bought for us to give out. Halloween and Easter were the only times during the year when we would have candy in the house. My brother and I would quickly devour any candy left within a week. I remember my mom throwing a Halloween party for us one year complete with apple bobbing, hot cocoa and marshmallows, candy apples and spooky music. The house was full of laughing, excited children all jostling for a better position in line to pin the tail on the donkey.

My mom was quite the hostess. Thanksgiving

was another one of those joyful planned events that we would go all out for. My dad also got involved by preparing any 8-tracks or cassettes for the parties. Mom would prepare a traditional Thanksgiving dinner and together they would invite family and friends. After dinner, the adults would retire to the basement. The children would stay upstairs playing board games and telling jokes and stories. There were usually about five kids, my brother and I included.

As we got older and styles and traditions of time changed, we would sit around and watch cable. Playing with the other children felt good...no, it felt right. I listened to the muffled sounds of music and boisterous laughter coming from the basement. Cards or 'bones' were slammed onto the bar accenting the fact that the one doing the slamming was winning the game. In a house filling with anger and criticism, I embraced moments like the ones experienced during holidays. Laughter, contentment, and peace reigned if only just for one day.

Of all the holidays, I loved Christmas the most. My parents received a Sears & Roebuck's catalog every year. During the time span between Thanksgiving and Christmas, my brother and I would sit and browse through the toy section, circling the toys we wanted in the naïve hopes that our parents would purchase everything we set our sites upon. I would ride with my dad into Washington DC to his preferred Christmas tree lot where he selected our tree. Once it was brought home and fitted into its stand at our bay window, the tree trimming would commence. My mom, my brother and I would precisely place colored balls, lights and tinsel on the tree. The final touch would be to spray it with artificial snow. For the grand finale, the lights were plugged in. All the other lights in the house got turned off and the family would stand around that tree, a feeling of awe washing over me to see our efforts twinkle and blink. Mom would also place one electric candle in each window all around the house. Dad went outside and hung lights that would blink intermittently.

Yes, we definitely showed the Christmas Spirit. After the windows were sprayed to mimic snowdrifts, garland was hung along the mantel above the fireplace complete with a stocking for each of us. The Christmas tablecloth was placed on our formal dining room table, topped with a ceramic cake stand that looked real enough to eat. Finally, with every ornament in place, our home was effectively transformed.

Presents would begin to appear under the tree. When our parents were not home, my brother and I could not contain our curiosity. We would carefully lift the tape securing the packages, dying to know what was inside. Careful not to rip the delicate wrapping paper on those mysterious boxes, we would totally expose and play with every toy. Knowing our parents could come home any minute, we would reluctantly put them all back exactly as they were. I guarantee my parents were never aware that we knew what every box contained by Christmas morning.

On the nights when I could not sleep, I would go downstairs to the living room, curl up in our big recliner with my quilt and watch the lights blink on the tree. The Christmas music my dad played during the day filled my mind. I recalled the tunes from the

Jackson Fives' Christmas Album, Lou Rawls, and Bing Crosby. I would watch the colors from those lights bounce, changing shape, colliding together on the walls, appearing to my childish imagination like tie-dye.

Christmas morning could not get there fast enough. After everyone finally pulled themselves from their beds and piled into the living room, presents would get ripped open with much fervor. If I were to evaluate each holiday and the feelings they evoked, I would say I loved them all but Christmas was definitely at the top of my list.

5

Usually, after living a day or a week stress free, a child's mind may forget about harsh criticisms or tasteless acts of bitterness – on the conscious level. Unfortunately, bliss did not last for too long afterward. I did not hear my parents argue frequently, but it happened often enough for me to recognize the commencement of one. My parents yelled so loud and with such rage and animosity. It felt as if I were standing at the receiving end of all that fury even though they always argued behind the closed doors of their bedroom.

As soon as I heard their door slam, I would run to the basement, into the furthest corner of the family room. Clinching my fists over my ears, music would deliberately fill my mind. Eventually, I would slide down the wall, ending up seated with my knees drawn to my chest. Sitting there, rocking back and forth, eyes squeezed shut, I would try to block out the sound and feelings of their arguments by humming loudly. Sometimes, an occasional word would reach my ears. My dad seemed to derive some sort of pleasure from calling my mom Jezebel. I can remember hearing that word quite often in several different arguments. I recently went to my reference bible and looked up Jezebel. She was described as being a wicked queen, revengeful, vein, a murderess, inciting her husband to evil. I can not see my mom in any of those contexts. My conclusion is he picked the worst character he could find and labeled mom with it just out of spite. A child cannot be repeatedly exposed to that kind of anger without it affecting him or her on some psychological level. It is inevitable that the consequences of those experiences will manifest themselves later in that life.

I slowly began going through a few changes of my own. Again, at the age of seven, my mom allowed us to use the community pool. In the short period of time that made up the beginning of the foundation of my life, I had already had a boy kiss me, had another one give me an experience I did not need, plus I had been exposed to intense bitterness and anger. When Chris returned to the pool and told me he had to show me something, I followed him without hesitation. When we reached the other side of the school, I asked him what was it that he wanted to show me. His quick response was, *This*, and he kissed me. Something was different this time. I kissed him back. To me, it was a real kiss – as real as it could get for a seven-year-old – with accompanying butterflies. After that summer, they never reopened the pool and I never saw Chris again.

My mom went through some changes, as well. Most changes were for the best. Some were not. For example, my mom used to drink. I remember watching her cook dinner with a glass of wine on the counter. Everyday, she would come home from work and fill her glass while preparing dinner, occasionally taking a sip. Also, mom was what I considered to be...let's just say she was a little loud with her opinion. Out in public, if she felt she had received inadequate service, she would definitely let the offending party know. She was not a soft-spoken, subdued woman. I assume she was not satisfied with her present character traits because one Saturday, in our dining room, she stated to me that she needed a change.

You know, sometimes we need to grow. I've got some baggage that I want out of my life. I don't like some things about myself and I'm going to change it.

...and from that moment on, she changed. No more wine while she cooked. Mom was still opinionated but there were not any more moments of her cursing at women in parking lots just because they backed out in front of her.

On the outside, we appeared to be the ideal, upwardly mobile family. We seemed to be the happy household. Outings to the best national parks, long Sunday afternoon rides across the country side. We even had dinner every evening at the formal dining room table complete with place settings and serving dishes. My dad liked to make sure we had a rich since of family and heritage. Sitting around the dinner table, he usually talked to us about his childhood, his family, and the property his ancestors owned. He always found a way to weave a logical point into his stories giving me a since of self-confidence and worth. A lot of what was said around that table helped to mold me into who I am and how I think. Those were moments when he was on the upside. The downside consisted of berating other families, pointing out how badly they were doing implying we were doing so much better.

Even though my parents were big on talking about family unity when discussing our heritage, I did not feel too much of that in our home. For example, my father would give me money or take me with him when he went places and, yes, it did make me feel special or important until he would bring up the subject of my brother or my mom.

Don't mention this to your mother or your brother (he rarely referred to Tyrone by his name when speaking to me). You know how they are. Your mother would make a big deal out of it and your brother is jealous of you anyway.

There just was not an atmosphere of loyalty in my house. I knew my dad gave me so much more attention then he gave my brother. The content of that attention became more than I desired.

6

My peers used to label me as goofy or silly. I was a very happy-go-lucky child. I did not fit into any mold or conform to the fads or styles of that era. I giggled a bit too much (in other peoples estimation), and was very animated when expressing myself. My mannerisms were not precisely the same as my peers and kids will notice and condemn everything that is different from the general populace. Even though my parents made sure we had a full, productive childhood, I still held a deep need to be noticed and accepted, for I knew and understood that I was indeed different. I guess you could say I craved more attention than what I already received.

Tonya! Guess what?

What?

I'm pregnant.

No you not! Stop lien'! How?

I did it. You know!

Girl, you stupid and that's nasty. I'm tellin'.

A few moments later, I was called over to the teacher's desk. She told me she did not need that type of garbage in her classroom and to report to the principal's office.

April, we don't understand what would make you say such a thing. It's not acceptable and we're calling your father.

I began to cry.

Please don't call my dad. I'll get a whuppin'.

You should have thought of that before you told such a story.

My dad showed up to get me. The office used to call my mom if there was a problem or sickness. In the midst of my mom *changing some things*, she changed the rules.

From now on, if there's a problem, you'll need to go to

your dad. If you need permission for something, go to him. He's the head of the house.

It had always been that anything my dad had said went, anyway. I believed my mom finally relinquished her say about any issue so the peace would be kept.

My dad and I walked across the street in silence. When we reached the house, he told me to go to my room. A silent foreboding settled over me as I waited for his call.

About one week prior to this, my class had earned a game of silent speedball. The game consisted of silently throwing the ball to another classmate until they talked, held the ball longer than two seconds, or dropped it. The teacher told us we had to stay quiet as we prepared to play and if someone spoke, we would lose our privilege. Well, someone spoke; therefore, we did not get to play the game. I was not happy. We were excused to go to the bathroom and while I was in there, I voiced my opinion about the whole thing, using a few colorful words. Someone told the teacher and when I returned to our classroom, I was sent to the office. This particular time, my mom came, for this incident happened before the new rule. When we got home, not without much sermonizing during the short walk crossing the street, she told me to write each curse word ten times. When my dad got home, she showed that paper to him. He looked at it and did nothing.

As I sat in my room wondering what would happen to me for these two trespasses, I was not prepared for what commenced. My dad called me into his bedroom.

You think you're grown?

No, sir.

Yes you do. You think you're gown. Since you want to act grown, I'll show you what it is to be grown.

My father told me to stand on his bed. I was an eight-year-old little girl and was nowhere near as tall as my six-foot tall father. He then kissed me as a man would have kissed his wife, not his baby girl.

You can't tell anybody about this. They would not understand. This is between you and me. I've been waiting for you to be ready and you've shown me that you are.

I went to my room in a daze, confused and scared. When I got there, I closed the door and lost control of my bowels. For years afterwards, I believed that if I had not gone to school and told such a story about being pregnant or if I were not as physically affectionate or if I had not kissed Chris, I would have never opened the door to the hell that became my life from that moment on.

My father had kissed me only once, during that first year. After I turned nine, he began kissing me more often, always when no one was home and with me standing on something to make me taller. Then it went from kissing to touching. One day, when I went for a ride with him, the content of his conversation lead to boys and how sneaky they are in their advances toward unsuspecting young ladies. As he pulled the car into the entrance of a deserted parking lot, he continued in his explanation of how to spot the different types of methods men use to deceive and beguile women.

You're getting older and boys are going to start noticing you. You need to be prepared for what they will say and do.

He then physically showed me in great detail. Afterwards, on the way home, he would give me the same old speech with small variances but the same meaning.

You're very grown-up for your age. I've never loved you as a daughter, only as a woman. You're special and our special relationship can't be talked about to other people. They wouldn't understand.

Even though, at times, my dad lavished me with good, wholesome attention, those times were becoming fewer and further between. I began building resentment against the abnormal relationship developing between my father and me. That resentment was evident one day when I had been told to rake the backyard. Our backyard was a good-sized area. I raked it in its entirety and was more determined then usual to do a really good job. When I had the job done, I came into the house, beaming, and told my mom,

Mom, I'm finished with the yard and I did my very best.

My mom usually showed enthusiasm about what came out of our mouths. She didn't critique that many of what I felt were achievements.

That's great, honey.

My father, however, had resorted to tearing down the magnitude of our accomplishments. It was irrelevant to me whether he did it for the purpose of holding the baton high enough to keep us reaching or for the sake of keeping our egos from swelling. As I stated, *I did my very best*, he walked into the kitchen and made a nonchalant comment, as he went to look for a snack in the refrigerator,

Sometimes, you best isn't good enough.

Instantly, the beaming smile faded from my face as I felt my pride in my achievement shrink into nothing. An unspoken thought sprang into my mind and heart with such veracity that I felt it course through my very soul.

I hate you and I can't wait to move out of this house.

I felt such a deliberate calm, a distinct purpose behind that thought until instinctively, I knew that I would work toward that specific goal.

7

Mom wasn't aware of the situation with my father. She had her own struggles and torment to deal with. One Sunday morning, we were preparing to go to church. My father never attended the services at our little Baptist church. Mom had packed a few suitcases and told my father she was taking some old clothes to charity. My brother and I had no reason to doubt her. The three of us piled into her little blue Volkswagen Beetle and off we went. Approximately fifteen minutes into our ride, my brother made an important observation.

This isn't the way we go to church.

My mother's reply was swift as if she had rehearsed it.

No it isn't. We're not going to church. We're going to Missouri to stay with your grandmother. I'm leaving your dad.

You should have heard the cheers going up in that car. I was so happy. I almost cried. My brother was equally as excited. We began to tell her of our woes given at our father's hand.

It was an eighteen-hour drive from Maryland to Missouri. My mom did not have any help to make that drive; therefore, we stopped in West Virginia at a hotel for the night. While we were there, mom called my father to let him know what our plans were. That night, we all had a peaceful night's sleep and in the morning, we were back on the road to grandmas.

I absolutely adored my grandmother. She was the typical all-American grandma. Be it at our home or hers, she always had sweets and treats even though she was an insulin dependent diabetic. I used to watch her give herself insulin shots each day. She never winced or showed any discomfort at doing it. She said she had gotten used to it. Don't get me wrong – grandma was far from the little old lady with the shawl, cane and white hair. My grandma was opinionated, aggressive and did not have a weak bone in her body. She definitely enjoyed entertaining and having company in her home, which is probably where my mom got the knack.

My grandfather also was great in my eyes. He would sit me on one of his thighs, my brother on the other and bounce us up and down, back and forth, jiggling us like Jell-O until our laughter filled the house. He always greeted me with a smile and, as though it was an afterthought, would then fish around in his pocket to retrieve a quarter for me. Whenever he left the house, I always pleaded to go with him. My grandfather was the only man that was close to me in my childhood that had never looked upon me with lust. He always had a twinkle in his eye. He kept his head smoothly shaven and he would let me rub his baldhead, giggling at the feeling of his head against my palm.

We always knew when we were close to grandmas: the Arch of St. Louis. It was a huge metallic landmark, catching the sun, ushering in the way from the East of The United States into the West. When I saw it, I knew we were less than a half hour from their house, even though it seemed like forever. As mom pulled the car into the driveway and we walked up to the front door, I heard the greeting I was sure we would recieve: grandma's toy poodle yipping excitedly from the other side of the door.

As soon as we were settled into our new environment, we were enrolled into school. Though I had never ridden a school bus before, I now rode one to and from school. This made me somewhat nervous at first. At the end of the first day, as the bus approached my grandma's house, I started gathering my belongings. The bus went past my house, continuing on down the street. I started to panic, thinking the bus driver had made an error.

Hey, that's my house! You're passing my stop!

Absolutely no one paid attention to my ranting. Within a few moments, I realized there was one localized bus stop where all of the children get dropped off and picked up. I felt silly about my outburst. After a week or so of building a routine and becoming adjusted to our new surroundings, I started to relax.

One day, while walking up to our driveway, I was basking in my newfound peace. That feeling of peace was slowly replaced by confusion, then a sinking disappointment as I saw my dad packing our luggage into the car. My feelings at that very moment were equivalent to a train being derailed and slamming into a brick wall. My mom met me in the yard and simply stated we were going home. That ride home was quiet and ominous.

8

We returned to our normal, daily routines a though nothing had ever happened. Creativity and curiosity helped my brother and I get through the turbulence in our childhood. Because Tessie was like a sister to the both of us, she aided in our creative process. I can remember a few events where the three of us got together to allow some of our imaginative juices to flow.

One such event was our carnival. Tessie, Tyrone, and I ordered a case of little give away items like bead ball games, fake watches, etc. We would make flyers, have mom make copies and we would post those throughout the neighborhood. Then would make cupcakes, cookies and have sodas to sell. Our final preparation would be to erect different decorated tables in Tessie's backyard. These were used to sell our refreshments or to have games where people could win the little trinkets as prizes. When the carnival was said and done, we had made about $20 each. That was a lot of money for a child to acquire in the early '80's'.

There was also the Metro bus and subway. For only a few quarters, we could ride the bus practically anywhere in Maryland or DC, and for a few quarters more, we could ride the subway into downtown Washington DC where we could spend the whole day going to all the museums. My favorites were the Smithsonian and the Air and Space Museums. We had talked Mrs. Hamilton into allowing Tessie to go along with us. We all arose early one Saturday morning and had spent the entire day in DC. That afternoon, when exiting the subway terminal to walk home, Tessie was a little short on her fare. The gate would not open unless we put the correct amount of money into the machine. Instead of helping her, we decided to play a prank. Tyrone and I waved at her then headed toward the escalators that went above ground. Tessie panicked. She had never ridden the Metro before. Tessie started hollering for us not to leave her, her cries and pleas falling upon deaf ears. We stood at the top of the escalator and waited for her out of her line of sight. When Tessie came above ground, her face showed a mixture of fear and anger. When she saw us laughing a few yards away, she was furious. She fussed at us for the duration of the walk to our homes. She told her mother about our 'joke' and she was never again permitted to ride the Metro with us.

As before, life resumed its normal course when

we returned form Missouri including my father's advances towards me. Within two or three weeks, he was back to showing me how to be wise to fresh boys. Soon he became more brazen with his acts as well as his reasoning.

You know, in the Bible, the father would lay with their daughters to bare them seed, continuing the blood line. Yeah, it was a natural, normal occurrence. Of course, you know not to say anything to your mother. She wouldn't understand. You and I have a special relationship, anyway. You're my best friend. I can't talk to anyone else the way I can talk to you. You are the only person that understands me. We'll make this the last time.

That statement - the using of the Bible as a legitimate reason to sexually molest me - planted a hatred and confusion about the role of church and the Bible on a psychosomatic level in my life. I did not consciously abhor the bible or Christianity. I only knew that particular belief system as an authoritative avenue - the ultimate truth to live by. Even though I felt within myself that this could not be right (the way my father justified his usage of the bible), I complied because of the authority of my parents (especially my father) as well as the ultimate authority of the church. It carried a certain finality with it. Whether I agreed or not was never an option.

Later in life, after it was all over, people would ask me why I had not told anyone when it started. My explanation is not too complicated. Look back at how my brother and I were raised. If we were told to do something, we did it, no questions asked, even if the demand seemed strange. I guess the fear of being whipped was not even the largest persuader. It was the way that my father stared us down anytime we were in trouble. My mom would tell him of the punishable act we had committed and before he would say a word, he would stare at which ever between us was the offender for at least twenty seconds or more. Count to twenty. That seems like eternity when all four family members were present and everyone watched you. It would be deathly quiet. A person is not able to comprehend the massive affect that has on a child. Heart racing, my insides would knot up. Finally, when the intimidation was over, I would have to beat a path to the bathroom. The fear was immense enough to loosen my bowels. There were several times when I did not make it to the commode, heaping humiliation on top of fear.

I cannot emphasize enough how children feel they are to blame for the abuse they sustain. My father had always told me how much more grown up I was above other children and how I had proven to him my readiness. Constant statements about my being ready plus the knowledge of how physically affectionate I had always been made me believe that if I had just not hugged and kissed him so much or if I would have been more resistant, all of this could have been prevented.

By the time I reached ten years old, I was being molested six or seven times a month. Even though I tried to stay away from my father, there were still those days when that unshakeable faith children have in their parents prevailed. I would venture out with him, not just hoping but fully believing that nothing bad would happen. After he had driven a considerable distance from the house he would pull the car over on the side of the highway and molest me as countless numbers of cars passed by. Other times, he would wait until my mom was upstairs in our house and he would molest me in the basement. My mind would scream as tears – always tears – slid down my face, *Can't anyone see what's going on in this car?* Or, *Why doesn't mom come downstairs? Please, mom, come down those stairs!*

The bait my father dangled before me was the attention he lavished on me. I was allowed to go everywhere with him. He would buy me ice cream or some other treat, bopping his head to the rhythm of whatever tune he had playing, tickling me in the crook of my neck, goading me to giggle, attempting to persuade me into having a more carefree attitude. I had begun my companionship with loneliness and distrust. I carried such a defeated attitude until he knew he would have to try harder to win my trust. Unfortunately, his bait was not the only factor working against me. Puberty came into play as well.

I was becoming physically and mentally aware of what was happening. Already quite developed, I had begun menstruating that year. My mind was beginning to comprehend what was happening and an incredible war was going on inside of my body. I was beginning to respond to his actions and that confused me. I instinctively knew that the advances from my father were wrong and - mentally, I hated it, but hormones and sensations that were fresh and highly sensitive were bombarding my body. This was another link in my chain of guilt.

Despite the feeling of guilt, despite fear of retaliation if I were to ever tell, and despite the constant brainwashing by my father, I finally told my mom. I do not remember her emotional response. What I do remember is her taking me to the police precinct. I had never been to a police station nor had I ever had any reason to be associated with one. When my mom and I walked into the station, I apprehensively looked around. Gray desks were neatly set up in rows. Police officers occupied each seat. As they observed us, pity briefly sparked in their eyes, then they resumed whatever they were doing before we came in. My mom must have phoned ahead. A female detective came into the front office as though she were expecting us. She asked me to follow her. In the back of the room was a door leading to a short hallway. Once in the hallway, we went into another room that was void of any furniture except a desk and two chairs. We went inside and as she closed the door, she introduced herself.

My name is Detective Ford. What I'm going to do is first ask you some questions which I want you to answer as best you can, okay?

Her voice was kind and understanding even though the questions she asked were frank. I felt naked in front of this perfect stranger. She eventually came to a question that I did not understand but was too ashamed to ask her to explain.

Were you sodomized or did your father ask you to

commit sodomy?

Now, mind you, this question was directed at a ten-year-old child. In my childish mind, I thought my father had made me commit every heinous act possible. Even though I never gave him oral sex, my response to the detective's question was *yes*. I did not know the definition of the word *sodomy* and the detective had not explained the act.

Once the thorough interrogation was over, she placed a pad of paper and a pencil on the desk in front of me and told me to write down everything my father did to me, in detail, and she then left the room. To sit there alone without any distractions and have to write every detail was a horrible experience for it brought each moment my father had touched me to the front of my mind. It was as though I were reliving it all over again. I could feel his hands, smell his cologne, see our surroundings and feel every sensation. I thought I was going to vomit. The police precinct ordeal took about two hours and when we walked out the door I had a headache. I was relieved that it was all over. Boy, was I wrong

Our next stop was at the clinic. I did not know what they would do or how it had anything to do with being touched by my father. A nurse finally called my name and my mom and I followed her into an examining room. I was told to take every thing off and to put on a gown. I was already feeling apprehensive and vulnerable and was not the least bit prepared for what was to commence. The doctor – a man – had me sit on an exam table, place my feet in stir-ups while scooting my rear almost off of the table, spreading my knees as far apart as they would go. Now here I am, a little girl who had been violated as it were and the humiliation and shame of being totally exposed to this man was overwhelming.

He then harshly proceeded with his pelvic exam. Blunt pains were stabbing through my body as well as my pride as I tried to scoot off of the table in the opposite direction from him. He abruptly stopped, gruffly told me to put my clothes back on and left the room, leaving me there confused, embarrassed and hurting. I hurriedly dressed then my mom and I waited in the doctor's consultation office. He finally came into the room and sat behind his desk.

Well, Mrs. Harris, her hymen is still intact. She's never been penetrated.

That is about all of that conversation I can remember. My head was buzzing with thoughts that somehow, I was being punished for telling. That's why that man hurt me. We left the clinic and went home.

As usual, life carried on, for a few days anyway. I was downstairs in the family room watching TV when my mom called me from the top of the stairs.

April, come upstairs for a minute.

I got up from the floor and ran upstairs, thinking she had some chore for me to do. When I reached the stairs and opened the door, I was not prepared for the atmosphere that I stepped into. My parents were seated together on the couch. I looked from my mom to my father and back to my mother, bewilderment keeping me gripped to the spot where I stood. My heart began beating so hard I could feel the roar of blood pulsating in my ears. When my parents saw they had my full attention, my mom began to speak.

Your father and I have been talking. Whatever happens in this house is our family's private business. We don't need to air our business before every Tom, Dick and Harry. Your loyalty should be to this family and it was wrong for you to bring charges against your own father. I don't know what possessed you to make such accusations about your dad but it ends now, is that clear?

I did not know how to respond. During that fraction of hesitation, I was experiencing more bewilderment about the fact that my mother just turned on me. I felt guilt, but I did not understand why because I knew I had told the truth. I definitely felt betrayed. During this entire lecture, my father just sat there staring at me with his eyebrows pushed up into his forehead giving me an expression that read, *Didn't I say you'd get in trouble?*

My only choice was to meekly nod in the affirmative. After my mothers' lecture on *privacy* and *loyalty* and how wrong *I* was, she made one final statement as she and my father left the room.

You need to have a seat and think about it. Maybe next

time, you'll think twice before accusing your father of such things.

I was totally flabbergasted as I sat there in the living room by myself, completely isolated. Yeah, I took time to think about it, all right! I thought about how if I had never told, would the repeated molestation by my father with it's embarrassment and feelings of disgust be more tolerable than being emotionally torn down and betrayed *once* by my mother. The loneliness finally got the best of me as I sat there and cried all by myself.

9

We had been attending a Baptist church near Pennsylvania Avenue in Washington DC. Potomac Baptist Church was a quaint little brown stone church with about fifty members. It had the traditional offices of deacons, ministers, elders, mothers, ushers, and of course, reverend. My mom was the piano/organ player. We had different choirs that sang during various services. I was a member of the children's choir and when I became old enough, I joined the junior usher board. I felt so important standing at the doors leading into the sanctuary.

We were members at Potomac from as early as I can remember. As a very small child, I would sit here, there, and then over there, where ever I thought I could talk someone's ears off. When I was a little girl and chose to sit with my mom, she would let me curl up in her lap. I can remember nodding off and then jumping as I was startled awake by a crescendo in the reverend's sermon. My mom would scoop me up, my right ear resting over her heart, with my bottom cradled in her lap and my legs dangling off to her right. One day, while I tried to get comfortable in mom's lap, I realized I was getting too big for this privilege. I just could not fit enough of myself into her lap nor could I position my right arm in a semi-hug around her left side without getting a crook in my neck. I do not believe I sat on her lap too often after that.

During our membership, I had been slowly growing in a friendship with a little girl who was the same age as me. Her name was Toni. She lived a couple of blocks from the church and as our relationship flourished, mom allowed me to spend the night with her and visa versa. One particular weekend, Toni stayed with me. Tessie came over to play as well. The three of us were in the middle of a game of Jacks when Toni thought of a different idea.

Hey, let's pretend we're shopping and each jack is a quarter and we can buy stuff. Oh, no. I know! Let's pretend we're all grown-ups. We could act like we're in cars driving!"

These ideas did not sit well with Tessie.

Grow up. Why can't we just play a game with real jacks right here on the real floor in the real world. We're too old to be pretending.

We were all old, decrepit preteens.

Tessie has always been very down to earth, kind of probing, and philosophical. Oh, don't get me wrong. She did go through the pretend stage. She, Monica, and I would pick out our favorite doll from our individual collections. Mine was a Baby Alive with a moving mouth, baby food and diapers for it was indeed capable of poo poo and tee tee. We would dress our dolls in their prettiest dresses then meet at Tessie's house for *brunch*. We would prepare triple decker ham and cheese sandwiches for only the finest restaurants served triple decker ham and cheese. With our glasses filled with grape soda- our favorite –, we would daintily sit at Tessie's formal dining room table with the chandelier lights dimly lit. We pretended to be in our twenties – of course – and had one little baby girl each. We talked grown up talk and chatted about how we would spend the afternoon.

Monica was the shy one. That shyness was apparent only around adults. When we were alone, she was as any other kid. During one of our brunches, she demonstrated the kid in her.

I heard this joke. Wanna hear it? Chinese, Japanese, dirty knees, look at these!

As she said, *these*, she gestured toward the area of her torso where her future development would reside. At that precise moment, Mrs. Hamilton walked into the dining room, hearing all, seeing all. Monica looked at Tessie. Tessie and I looked at Monica. Time froze for a brief moment, each of us waiting for Mrs. Hamilton to climb all over us. She raised an eyebrow in mock surprise, a glint of humor playing around her eyes.

Monicaa! I didn't think you had a vooice. You're usually so shy and quiet. I would have expected that from them, not yoouu. That was so cute. Chinese, Japanese, dirty knees, look at theeese.

Tessie's mom had the inherited trait of drawling the last word of her sentences. She was one of the sweetest women I knew and I loved to hear her talk. She had skin the color of caramel and the most beautiful wavy, long hair. I used to equate her hair with the rolling waves of the ocean.

Monica's mother was equally as sweet. Whenever Tessie and I went to their house, Mrs. Spann always seemed so pleased to see us. It was her trademark to feed us. When I walked into her kitchen, I always knew what drink would be in the refrigerator – lemonade. It was lemonade when I was a kid and lemonade after I was grown and had a child of my own. Tessie, Monica and I rode bikes together, played with dolls together and shared every secret imaginable. As I grew older, they became my sunshine in an ever-growing storm.

10

In the fifth grade, my music teacher surprised me. She asked me and two other students to join the county chorus. The Prince Georges County Chorus was a choir consisting of about 200 children handpicked from various schools throughout our county, joining to form one voice. I do not know if my being picked was honestly due to my vocal ability or because my mom was a fellow music teacher. I really do not want to know. Let me go on believing that I was above average, spectacular and that my music teacher saw something worth savoring.

This choir was a source of peace. When all hell was breaking loose in my life and home, music was comforting. My father had gone back to molesting me within one month of my bringing charges against him.

I believe a truly abusive personality is predictable. If this is a fact then my father's next move was right on the mark. I had always been told to be home within an hour of going to a friend's house, so as not to wear out my welcome. After bringing up charges against my father, anytime I asked to spend the night at a friend's house, the answer was now a swift, unexplained 'no'. I began missing my own best friends' birthday sleepovers. By cutting back on the amount of time I could spend with my friends, he affectively eliminated the chance of my giving away our secret. Then one day when I was twelve, my father came home with the news that he had found a great church and we were to be going there starting that following Sunday. This further isolated me and placed me in an environment where I was a total stranger. No more Toni.

During this time of transition, I started receding into a shell. Little by little, the bubbly, carefree, always smiling April gave way to a more subdued, insecure introvert. I started gaining weight and spending more time by myself. As the molesting reached once or twice a week, I increased my effort to stay away from my father. If my mom went somewhere, I wanted to be right by her side. If my father were late getting home from work, I would hope and pray that he had been in a car wreck and killed. I had always found refuge in fantasizing, thus I began to resort more often than not to living within the recesses of my mind, my imagination. It was becoming the only peace that I had. I tuned out my environment and became so wrapped up in my mental skits that my outward expressions depicted what was taking place in my mind. I reveled

in the very idea and mental picture of balling up my
fist and with all of the anger, rage, hurt and shame
fueling its' momentum, I slammed it into my father's
face, sending bone fragments and blood everywhere.

In the second grade, after that first incident with
my father, our class was asked to write a poem about a
place where we would like to go and to describe it in
detail:

I wish I could go to a deserted island.
I would lie on the sand and watch the
Moonbeams play atop the water like
Pearls on the bay. Quiet. Alone. The
Sun would be my orange and I would
Eat its rays of life.

All of that was not from my mind but from my
eight-year-old heart. I no longer complained when my
mom sent me to walk the three blocks to the store.
Any solitude, any moment away from my father and
my home, satiated my desire for peace. Squinting my
eyes at the kisses from the wind, I embraced nature;
life. No more subliminal fingers of fragmented thought
entangling my experience of the present moment. The
natural environment was so beautiful to me. It was raw,
untainted, and breathtaking. Nature represented the
right order of things. It did not present any threat of
deviating from that order. Once we inhabit this human
host, our spirit will always yearn for the return to
that primordial stillness, peace, and pervading truth

untainted by human experience or thought. That yearning can be interpreted as a quest for God or the return to God's presence. As I continually experienced religious indoctrination, that tradition – the quest for God – was deeply imbedded in my consciousness. Church was the path taken by my family as we attempted to travel towards God.

The Sunday for us to attend the new church finally arrived. Even though I had been in church since a baby, I had no definition for the concept of God. I was curious as to why I had never felt or perceived God in my little church, but I did feel that heightened sense of exhilaration when we went to one of the sister churches our congregation used to visit. To me, God was an entity who created everything, masculine in nature, and all knowing, all powerful. I had never experienced, talked to, nor heard from God for myself. As we walked into the welcome area of the new church that Sunday morning, I was thinking to myself that this church was no different from any other. That sentiment changed when we went through the double doors leading into the sanctuary. All of a sudden, I felt a sweet, subtle euphoria envelop me. I believe it was God's presence evoked by the unified beckoning and unwavering expectance of the people.

After analyzing that unique feeling, only then was I able to take in the scope and layout of the sanctuary. It was large, probably seating 500 people. There were three columns of pews with at least 15 rows of pews in each column. There were people scattered throughout the sanctuary, praying in hushed voices. Quiet instrumental music played softly in the background.

I had never heard everyone praying aloud all together before. My first thought was how distracting it seemed, and yet, that pervading presence was tangible.

From that first service and on, I could not wait for each Sunday morning, Sunday evening and Thursday evening to come. As we walked through those double doors into that sanctuary, I was never disappointed. The sweet feeling of peace was palpable! Even at the age of twelve, I wanted to know more about the power I felt, therefore, I paid close attention to what was preached. What I heard mostly was if sinners were not baptized in the name of Jesus and if they were not filled with the Spirit of God and it be evidenced by speaking in a holy language that was induced by God, those sinners would go to hell when they died. The pastor, better known as the Bishop, would also give details about hell, the lake of fire, total separation from Jesus, being continually in utter darkness, falling, falling, and falling some more for eternity. After hearing this preached during several different services, I was petrified and within that first month, I asked for baptism. I now understand that this particular method of attempting to reach people does not produce fruit of love, patience, and compassion within one's heart. It does not create understanding and inner stillness. Fear seemed to be the catalyst that propelled people to obey the rules set by the church. In this way, the church was no different to me from my parents.

When I was first informed about our change to the Greater Scripture Church, my initial feelings were bitter. I believed my father was pulling me away from my friend, Toni, and I really did not want to change churches. However, after we continued to go there, I started making friends, getting involved and enjoying this new environment. I had never been a popular child but at least at church, I got along with everyone. One particular member stood out as a mentor for the young people. Vicki Woods formed a cheerleading squad and enjoyed sponsoring or coordinating various activates focusing on the youth. Her goals and desires were to have a close-knit safe haven for all the children and teenagers in attendance. She was an advocate for unity and loyalty. I appreciated her friendship, which was much needed in my life, especially at that time.

While we were attending Scripture, my father did something that was the most divesting event to befall a girl. He was still molesting me. Because of my ripe figure, I began to wear a large bulky robe around the house to cover myself. My father would watch me, devouring my chest or backside with his eyes whenever we were within the same proximity. It did not matter if someone else was present in the room or not. I harbored resentment toward my mom. I just could not believe she did not notice - did not even suspect - that something inappropriate was going on in her house. I stayed in my room a lot or if my mom went upstairs for any reason, I tried to find an excuse to go as well. An incredible conflict went on inside of my mind. If my father went somewhere, the little girl wanted to accompany her daddy, hoping nothing bad would happen. The older, bruised preteen wanted no part of him. Usually, the little girl prevailed.

One Saturday, my mom had errands to run and had left the house early before I even awoke. I did not have a chance to escape my father. I thought our house was large enough to sufficiently avoid him. Unfortunately, this was never the case. On Saturdays, he would lie on his bed and watch TV. He wore a terry cloth robe with nothing underneath. I could sense his restlessness. My presence was as a magnet drawing his advances. He would start pacing like a caged animal stalking its prey. After an hour or so of battling his internal demons and losing the battle, he would call me into his room and tell me to sit on the bed and watch TV with him. The little girl would comply, making sure not to sit too close, praying a mile a minute that this time would be different. It never was, except this particular time. It was worse, much worse. Usually he would tell me to take off my clothes and I would only take off the outer layer, trying to show my reluctance or noncompliance. He would remove everything else. I cried each and every time. I absolutely hated it and I hated him!

Since the age of eleven, his advances had become more intimate; each time going a little further until eventually, he took my virginity. As I had explained previously, my body was full of new hormones and heightened sensations. My father capitalized on that fact. That day, my body reacted in the fullest possible way to sexual stimulation. Instantly I felt empty and used. When it happened, I felt devastated, like I was spoiled, ruined. Not only had he stolen my virginity, which was monumental in itself, but I felt he had taken it all. Such a complete guilt gripped me at having aloud this ultimate violation to occur. I thought, *Well, I must have wanted him or my body would never have reacted.* Children do not understand human physiology. Some body functions and responses are instinctive and natural to certain stimuli. The way my body responded to my father's stimulation was not by my choice or any hidden, suppressed desire for him. It was a physiological reaction; nothing more.

When this appalling act was almost over, he asked me was I 'finished' so he could 'get his'. This became his practice each time. I would always cry, but that never stopped him. I was not just hurt, I was mad!

11

Life did not go on as usual. I had had enough! I hesitated for one week before I told my mom. The scenario from the first time I exposed him was still fresh. I remembered experiencing the denial, betrayal, punishment and ostracism. I was afraid; nevertheless, I did not care enough about those consequences to allow this to happen to me ever again.

We had been attending Scripture for a year and one particular Sunday morning, my parents had used separate cars because my mom had errands to run after that morning's service. Of course, I opted to ride with my mom. We had been driving down the road en route to her first errand, when I started contemplating telling her - but how? What would I say? Boy was I nervous! Knots were forming in my stomach and I knew if I did not go ahead and tell her, I would lose my nerve, hence losing my brief window of opportunity. I blurted it out.

Mom, it's started up again.

What's started up again?

Dad. He's messin' with me.

Silence.

I believe you. It was God that had us take separate cars this morning. We're turning around and we're going to talk with the Bishop. I've got to get you out of that house.

I had not felt that kind of rush in so long until I thought I would be overwhelmed. I was exhilarated, feeling total relief. By my mom going to the ultimate authority in our lives – the Bishop, a representative of God - I thought that it would finally be over. No more awkward moments. No more nasty feelings. I am free!

When we arrived back at the church and entered into the sanctuary, everyone was gone except for the Bishop and a few ministers taking care of after service business. I took a seat on the back pew while mom went to the Bishop's office door and apprehensively knocked. He said for her to enter, which she did, closing the door behind her. I was left alone in that huge sanctuary. I thought, *What if the Bishop doesn't believe me? Why does it have to be a man that I tell? Is this finally over?*

Each time my father molested me, he would say that it was the last time. Obviously, I could not take his word. With my not being believed by anyone I had confided in, plus my father's deception, I was incredibly insecure. I doubted peoples' word and my own ability to accomplish anything significant.

A moment or so went by and my mom returned to the sanctuary. I went with her into the Bishop's office, my heart pounding. We sat in two chairs facing his desk. He proceeded with, what I perceived as another interrogation. He asked me to explain what had happened. He then asked some very direct questions about how, where, what body parts, everything. After he had questioned me thoroughly, he agreed with my mom about us not returning to our home. The Bishop then called his mother-in-law, and arranged for us to stay with her for a few days. That would give us time to figure out what to do next. I was happy with this arrangement. She had six granddaughters whose ages ranged around my own.

I do not remember where my brother was during this time. There was so much going on inside of me and so many new arrangements were being made for my life. My head was reeling. Tyrone and I did, however, end up at Bishop's mother-in-law's home that very day, that night, and every subsequent night for a short period thereafter. The three of us slept in one large bedroom. My mom slept in one bed with my brother and I sharing another.

The next morning, I received a phone call.

April? Hey, this is Bishop Long. I have your father here with me. What I'm going to do is put the three of us on what's called a conference call. Your father will hear everything you say. Everything we say will be heard by you, okay?

Okay.

Tell me what you believed happened between you and your father.

Again, for the third time in my life, I had to recant the horrific accounts of what happened. After I'd said everything, Bishop Long spoke.

Now, Larry, why don't you state your side of the story.

Instantly, my ears and guard went up. Why was this Bishop calling him 'Larry' and not Brother Harris? Within the split second of my hearing his first name, I quickly deduced that my father had manipulated the whole situation to be in his favor. I had a good idea about what he was going to say. I was disappointed that my instincts were correct.

Well, Bishop, I don't know what she's talking about. I don't understand why she's making up this lie. She's mentally unstable and I believe she needs psychiatric help.

I was incredulous! My head was spinning from

the impact of his words and from the realization of where this was going. Again, I felt cornered, like I was the guilty party. When the Bishop spoke, I was at a loss for words.

April, do you have anything to say?

No. It happened and I don't know what else to say.

Okay. We'll be in touch. Bye.

...and he hung up. When I put down the phone, I was shaking. This adrenaline reaction had become my natural response to confrontation ever since my father started staring us down, boring his eyes through my soul. Again, I felt alone. I stood in the doorway between the living room and dining room dealing with what had just happened and the magnitude of my hopelessness, all by myself. After about a minute, I quit shaking, got myself togther, put on my, *everything is OK,* face and went on.

During our stay there, I was extraordinarily happy. The girls and I played double dutch, went for long walks, and sat up talking and laughing at night in our pajamas. It was like a grand slumber party. I lost 10 pounds that week. I assumed my mother was making some sort of alternative lodging plans for herself, my brother and I. Remembering the speech about not taking your own family into court, I thought she and Bishop Long had come up with something else. This was not the case. A few days later, mom packed up our meager belongings again, and told us we were going home. I did not understand. I thought safety and justice were supposed to rain down from the man of God, especially since we were residing in the household of his mother-in-law. When this was evidently not the case, I took it as another blow against my desire to trust people, especially family or anyone associated with the church.

After we had returned home, I was treated like a troublemaker. Ostracized, again. One morning, a few days after our return home, I asked my father for lunch money. He glanced at me with those raised eyebrows and spat, "Pst, ha! No." The guilt and feelings of betrayal came to a head at that moment. As my heart took another direct hit, I made up my mind to do what I should have done a long time ago. I had had enough.

12

I believed no one was on my side; therefore, I was going to have to find a way to prove that my father was indeed molesting me. My father started taking me to hotels. Eventually, he settled into repeatedly taking me to the same one. Usually he would stop for gas or at the liquor store, as it had become his practice to be moderately liquored up before molesting me. Discreetly pulling out tissue, gum wrappers, or anything available to write on, I would hurriedly scribble down where we were and whatever road signs or landmarks I saw. Only after cautiously peeking about, would I quickly and carefully shove the hastily written information down into my sock. I was definitely planning on turning him in to the police but I wanted to make sure I had so much evidence, no one could refute it. Hopefully, he would be thrown, not just into jail, but *under* it. Unfortunately, my efforts would take longer then I had anticipated to reap the desired results.

As stated before, usually each summer, my family took a weeklong summer vacation in Mississippi for our family reunion. I had also mentioned that it was a time of peace and happiness. This sanctity, however, was desecrated. The level of peace in my home continued to erode. Some time after our return from Mother Lee's house, we were scheduled to take our traditional vacation. My parents had been arguing quite often but keeping with a child's logic, I automatically assumed we would still go on vacation. I was partially correct.

My father had not recorded any traveling music. This should have sent warning bells ringing in my head, but it did not. If something occurred in our home which was abnormal, it was frequently overlooked, inadvertently sending the message that those events were acceptable. I did not feel any misgivings about my father not preparing any music for our trip. My mom had even packed our bags. The next morning, I woke up and prepared as I normally did for vacation. My dad told me to come on. Confused, I headed out the door to get into the car. As I looked over my shoulder, I saw my mom crying at the front door, waving at me. A slow understanding crept into my mind. My worst nightmare had come true. I was leaving the state, for at least a week – ALONE – with this man!

We pulled away from the curve, my heart still behind us on the sidewalk. I could not believe this was happening. Instantly, I was mad at God. *What had I done to deserve this? Why, God, do you hate me so* *much?! I must be the most vile, despicable creature on the planet. I am being toyed with and teased just to see how far I can be pushed before I go careening over the edge. Why me? I do not understand. **Why me?! I don't understand? IT'S NOT FAIR!!***

I quickly reined it in, got my state of mind in check and put on my *everything is OK* face. I knew I had to act the part of the happy, content daughter. My father had already told me, several times, that if I did not walk around the house in a large bathrobe, always trying to cover-up, or if I did not always try to avoid him or put him off, it would never have continued happening. He claimed I was giving him a challenge by constantly defying him. Each time he raped me – that is exactly what I considered it to be – he would not quit until I complied exactly how he wanted me to comply. I had to put my arms around him and answer all of his sensual questions he would whisper in my ear, adding shame to the assault by not just making me participate in the first place, but by demanding my total compliance and submission in the most manipulative way possible.

As we continued on our long drive, I carried on as though nothing was wrong, hoping I would return home after our *vacation,* untouched. We visited Mississippi, as well as Chicago. When we arrived in Chicago, I recalled people asking my father why my mom and brother were not there. I do not remember his response. I was just relieved no one asked me. I did not have to formulate a reply. Actually, during our entire trip, I can remember only one focal point.

My father has children from a previous marriage.

One sister in particular was closer to my family than the other siblings were. Her name is Theresa. During our trip, my father and I visited one of his sisters. He was not expecting Theresa to be there. Theresa had been hostile towards him for reasons of her own. Their reunion was not a desired one, so he dropped me off and said he would be back later. While he was gone, Theresa and I became reacquainted. After much small talk, laughter and idle chitchat, her demeanor changed as well the conversation.

April, is he messin' with you?

Boom! Where did that come from and why? I stumbled in my customary *everything is fine* façade. She must have sensed my hesitation in answereing such a blunt question. Finally, I stated,

Well, what am I supposed to do about it? I live in his house. I have to deal with him everyday and no one believes me, anyway.
Her answer was a concrete depiction of her personality.

Stand up to him! Tell him no.!

Our conversation went on for a little while longer. I was beginning to feel a surge of courage. I felt confident enough to stand up against my father, not only because Theresa said I should, but because she told me, she had my back. I *never* had anyone stand in my corner before and I was determined to capitalize on that moment.

When my father came back to get me, Theresa made a comment directed towards him, something to the affect of not liking her present company. Then - she left me. My confidence dwindled. My father and I also left and went back to the hotel.

Relief enveloped me upon noticing we had a room with separate beds. My father sat down on his bed and I turned on the TV, beginning to feel those slow pangs of anxiety. He then asked me to sit on his bed beside him and watch TV. He was seated near the head of his bed. I sat at the opposite end, trying to put as much distance between us as possible. The battle of wills began.

Come sit closer to me.

I scooted a little. He looked at me, sighed, and then moved to where I sat. He started stroking my leg. My skin began to crawl, the sensation of bile pressing at the base of my throat. I thought, "Ok, April. It's now or never." I pushed his hand away, got up from that bed, and stood, facing him.

What if I say 'No'?

Look, don't let your sister get you hurt. The more you resist, the harder it's going to be on you. I'm gonna get what I want. It's just a matter of how you go about giving it to me. Don't make me take it, now come over here.

I stood my ground, my heart pounding, defiance

etched in my face. In that instance, he changed. The next thing I knew, I was being grabbed and flung onto the bed. Still, I would not comply.

I will hurt you. Now take your clothes off before I rip them off, my self!

This man was a few inches from my face, bruising my wrists, half hissing, half spitting those venomous words. I was scared to death. Crying, I took off my clothes. I tried to hide my shame by climbing under the covers, pulling them tightly under my chin. While I had hurriedly undressed, my father was undressing as well. When he turned around, he became further enraged by my unyielding posture.

Like a savaged beast, my father ripped the covers out of my hands and away from the bed in one quick sweep, totally exposing my trembling body. A whirlwind was growing in intensity as he grabbed my legs and wrenched them apart. I heard roaring in my ears escalating into a crescendo. He was on top of me, crushing my breath away. Demon eyes, breath heated from hell on my face. Then – blank.

Sobs wracked my body when the rape was over. I went into the bathroom to clean myself, scrubbing until I was raw. My mind began to recede. No more pain. The sound of running water began to fade. Colors merged. From that moment until I was back at home and in my room was blank. Did he rape me again while we were still on *vacation*? I do not know. Did we visit any other states? What did I do while I was there? Where did we go? Whom did I see? I do not know. I had retreated into my safe haven within the realm of fantasy. I could have been in a den full of starving, salivating lions, about to be attacked and devoured, and I would never have known, would not have even flinched. Blank.

13

Fall came and school started. Those were the only new happenings in my home. My mom was still in denial about what I perceived as a demon living within our home, even though that spirit took several opportunities to rear its head. It lurked in every corner, watching and waiting for that precise moment to further oppress us. That opportunity continually rose in my brother's life as well as my own. My brother and I were close. That was slowly stripped from us over the course of our childhood. By the time I was nine or ten I tolerated him. That tolerance developed into indifference by my teenage years. I can remember an incident when my father walked in on a minor spat between my brother and me. His offhanded comment, as he walked through the room, was most uncalled for.

April, if he's bothering you, just pop him in the mouth.

I felt my brother's embarrassment from a place far beyond my cold heart. I did not feel empowered at all by my father's advice. Instead, I felt more shame for my brother.

It seemed to me that my father hated my brother. Now, as I look back, I have come to understand that his actions were an emotional manifestation of his own mental torments wrought from a painful past. I believed my brother felt the awful air in our home just as I did. He just responded differently. Tyrone did not make the best grades in school. The first marking period after that horrendous summer, my brother brought home a bad report card. My father used that as an excuse to unleash his own internal fury. He told Tyrone that he would get a whipping every day until the next report card. True to his word, every evening, within five minutes of my fathers' entering the house, I would begin to hear the horrible, pitiful screams escalating into pleas for mercy as that leather belt or extension cord tore into Tyrone's flesh, leaving long lasting, huge, swollen whelps. Every day, I would run to the basement to cower in my corner. With my hands clinched over my ears, my knees drawn to my chest, I would rock back and forth, humming loudly, squeezing my eyes shut. This went on for one week.

That following Sunday, we all dressed for church as usual. As the family proceeded out the front door, my brother pulled the door closed behind us. My father turned to Tyrone and asked where did he think he was going. My brother, standing there in his three-piece suit, looked puzzled. He stated he was going to church. My father then told him that he was not going to church, but instead, was to finish their project of painting the house.

My house was a two-story brick house with wooden shutters on the fifteen or so windows and a very large wooden bay window. My brother was fifteen or sixteen years old at the time. He just stood there in disbelief that our father would not only make him finish that paint job that they had started the day before, but the larger insult was he had waited until we had all walked out the front door. There was no way for Tyrone to re-enter for he did not have a key. Tyrone was humiliated at having gotten dressed in his 'Sunday's best' only to be expected to paint the house in those very clothes. Again, I felt my brother's shame so emphatically until it felt as though this act had been perpetrated against me. Crestfallen, Tyrone watched us go as my father, my mother and I walked to the car and headed on to church.

That afternoon, we returned to an empty house. I knew immediately that my brother had run away. It became evident by that evening, definite by the next morning. He was gone for close to six months. When he did return, my father called him to the basement. They were down there for more than an hour. I never knew what went on until fifteen years later. My brother informed me that our father placed a gun on the bar and over the coarse of that long ago hour, made it quite clear that Tyrone would sign up for the armed services. If not, my father would kill him. By concealing the weapon, my father was able to escort Tyrone out of the house without my or my mother's knowledge of the grim reality surrounding what was happening. During their ride, the gun laid menacingly on the seat between them as a constant visual reminder of his threat.

Life presumed its normal course. My brothers' feelings and mine came to rest in the same sentiment, a perpetual state of loathing for our father. Tyrone's feelings were bred from the constant unrelenting berating and unnecessary beatings inflicted against him. Mine were from the frequent sexual encounters. A void was continually wedged between my brother and me.

One of my brother's emotional outlets was his knack for creativity. He formed a club that I now am unsure of the subject matter, but he had scheduled a meeting one evening at a school's youth center for anyone interested. I was going to be a part of his club. Excited and pumped, my brother and I jumped into my father's car and off we went. When we pulled in front of the school, my brother sprung out of the car, excited about his personally conceived endeavor. As I opened my door preparing to follow him, those same ominous words my brother and I had heard before came from my father.

Where do you think you're going?

I looked at him, then my brother and I exchanged bewildered yet knowing glances as I haltingly answered that I was going into the school with Tyrone. Of course his response which we already knew what it would be, was no, I was not going with him or anywhere else with him. With much anger, I got back into the front passenger seat of the car and watched my brother slowly turn, bow his head, and walk towards the school. Again, I felt his feelings of rejection, embarrassment, and shame, which only served in fuelling my own loathing toward our father.

As we pulled away from the curve to head home, I guess my father felt some need to explain his actions. Maybe he felt the prevailing bond between my brother and me as well as the icy disdain flowing from my spirit towards him. I do not know, but he then add fuel to the fire by saying how much better I was than Tyrone and how I should raise my sights on things higher than anything that my brother could produce. He also believed my brother's club would flop anyway and he was just saving me from the downfall that he felt was inevitable. After he had finished slandering Tyrone, there was not anymore conversation. My brother was made to walk the twelve or more blocks home that night.

14

A few Sundays later, there was to be a youth meeting after morning service. Our parents allowed us to stay. I always felt relief when my parents were away. This seems to be a normal feeling among teenagers as they climb that ladder of life toward adulthood and independence. However, my sense of relief came from not only relishing in the short periods of independence but from knowing that, for a time, I would not feel threatened by my father. I would not experience the confusion and betrayal of my mother always siding with him. I believe my brother shared the same feelings. Though we did not talk often, we still could empathize with each other.

Our parents had always held a strict code of conduct over us. During church services, we had to sit within the first four or five rows of pews and that only included the two inside sections of pews out of the four sections in the church. After services, my parents usually made a straight beeline for the car and we had better be close on their heels. We were not to go anywhere without asking for permission, including to the grocery store that was directly across the street from the church. I now understand that a lot could happen to a kid in Washington DC, especially that particular area of Northwest DC. Most of the time, I avoided asking if I could go anywhere with the other church kids because it usually entailed a lengthy interrogation that only ended with a resounding, No.

Shortly after our parents left, we found out the youth meeting had been canceled. My brother called home. While we waited for one of my parents to come retrieve us, I decided to run across the street to buy a soda. I figured I had more than enough time before someone came to get us. I knew I was not supposed to go because our code was still enforced, even if our parents were not present. If they were not there to give permission then we knew we did not have the OK to proceed with anything. Upon my arrival back at the church, everyone said I had just missed my parents by not even thirty seconds. I knew it would take them some time to get home. I anxiously waited approximately a half an hour before I phoned home.

When I did call, my mom answered the phone. Her first question was where had I been. When I informed her of my whereabouts, she momentarily put the phone down to tell my father of my insubordinate act. When she came back to the phone, she told me my father

82

said to walk home and they had better not see me in someone's car.

Now, see if you can comprehend this. The church was in NW Washington DC, smack in the middle of a drug and prostitute infested area. I lived in Coral Hills, Maryland. It was a good twenty minute drive, so for me to have walked could have easily taken me two or three hours. By this time, it was five pm or better with the sky beginning to show an evening pinkish hew. I could have been mugged, raped, or killed before I would have ever reached my house.

This...*craziness* was a last straw. There was no way that man could abuse me repeatedly, expect me to keep my mouth shut about it and then expect me to cordially walk home. No way! Let us just see how he feels about being exposed again. I stalked around that church in search of that very same pastor that let him off the last time. I did not feel I needed him to side with me or believe me for I had something better than my word. I had evidence!

I had finally found the Bishop, pulled him to the side away from everyone and told him of what was happening again. He, in turn, found one of the sisters, and relayed the information to her. She then called child protective services. She came back to where I had been seated and told me of our course of action.

April, the social worker on the phone said you need to go down to the police station and give a statement. I'll take you and be a support for you.

We went straight to the police station where I

gave another two-hour report. Afterwards, the police officer had Sis. Mathis take me to a children's safe house. A counselor from *Safe Haven* greeted us at the door. I told Sis. Mathis *thank you*, then followed the counselor into the dining room. Taking a seat, we then went over the house rules.

We rotate the chores between the girls. If you cooked dinner today then tomorrow you'll wash the dishes and someone else will cook. We rise at 6:00 a.m. every morning and no one is allowed on the phone for more than 10 minutes. This home was designed to keep girls safe from whatever abusive situation they came from, therefore, no one is to know where you are or how to get here and you will not be given the phone number. Do you understand?

Sure, I understood. I understood that the shelter seemed like a prison. By now, it was ten or eleven at night and I was in desperate need of a bath. By this stage in my life, I had critically low self-esteem. I would go twenty or thirty days without bathing. I still had on my church clothes, which I had worn since seven or so that morning and by that evening, I smelled very bad. The shelter was not able to provide a change of clothes for me and no one was aloud to bring me any. I shared a room with three other girls and that night, I went to sleep in tears.

15

We were awakened the next morning at 6:00 a.m. sharp. The shelter was not able to supply me with a toothbrush. I 'washed my teeth' as well as my body with a washcloth although it did not help because of my previous lack of good hygiene. I still wore the same clothes from the last twenty-four hours. I was very pleased when they allowed Sis. Mathis to bring me clean clothes that evening, however, I had to wear the same clothes during that day. I did not think they would make me go anywhere in my present state. I was wrong.

I am unclear about the way the system works. I assume the authorities check to see if I have an existing file on record because that morning detective Ford showed up to take me to the same precinct where my original complaint was filed several years before. By her demeanor, I felt she was giving me a cold shoulder. My feelings were confirmed when I walked through the doors into the precinct. Everyone looked up to see who walked through those doors. Their looks of curiosity turned into icy glares. I was confused as to why they were all treating me with such disdain. Detective Ford and I walked into an empty office where she plopped a pad of paper and a pencil down on the table before me. She flipped a comment my way, never once looking at me. She walked out, in an air of boredom, closing the door behind her.

You know the procedure.

Why was everyone treating me so harshly? I incorporated that accusatory energy in the room into my psyche, further reinforcing my belief that the molestation was my fault. After I filled out yet another statement, Detective Ford came back to interview me. Once the interview was over, she finally exposed the root behind her attitude.

Do you know what a lie is?

Of course. It's something that's not true.

I'm asking because of several reasons. The last time you were here, you were asked if your father ever committed sodomy on you and visa versa. You had said yes, but now you're saying no. Also, you had dropped the charges giving the impression you had fabricated the entire story. Even when you pressed charges yesterday, it was in retaliation for your father making you walk home. Now do you want to tell me what's really going on because I don't have time for games.

Anger and resentment boiled inside of me. I was not thinking any longer. I was feeling.

First of all, how do you expect a ten year old to know what sodomy means? You never explained it, nothin'! I'm fifteen years old now. The only reason I know now is because I asked a friend. Second of all, I dropped those charges because my mother told me to and third of all, my anger towards my father was the only thing powerful enough to make me press charges, so don't sit there lookin' down your nose at me. I'm the victim.

That detective just looked at me. She finally asked how this time would be any different from the last. I told her this time was indeed different for I had proof. I knew where he had been taking me.

It had been a long day, therefore, Detective Ford said she would come and get me the next day so we could find that establishment. When we arrived back at the shelter, the detective reminded me of our trip to find that hotel the next day. I nodded and then walked inside. The counselor greeted me, informing me that Sis. Mathis had dropped off some clothes. I do not think I could have reacted any faster. Grabbing those clothes, I dashed for the bathroom to happily take a shower. Afterwards, I changed clothes then found a book to read. That day had indeed been a long day.

Before long, I was nodding off. After dozing for a little while, I ate dinner with the group, washed the dishes, and went to bed.

Laying there in the dark, one of the girls began to cry. Another girl coaxed her into talking about her problem. Between sniffles, she described her day in court, and how she was now, officially, a ward of the state. One by one, with the added comfort and privacy of darkness, each girl gave an account of how they had landed in the shelter. My story was not anymore outlandish then theirs and we quickly created a fragile bond, even if the bond was evident only during the nights when we shared a common room and a common darkness.

16

The next morning, detective Ford came to get me. We went on a hunt for that telltale motel. Unfortunately, I did not have my tissues and gum wrappers to guide us. For the first forty-five minutes, we fumbled around, being lead only by the bits and pieces in my memory. I would remember a portion of a route number or a specific landmark. Little by little, we made our way toward that place. Just as the detective gave a sigh of frustration, I looked out the passenger side window and there it was. I became excited.

Hold it! Hold it! That's it! That's the place!

There it loomed, exactly as I had described it, from the colors of the building and shutters all the way down to the shabby white chow chow dog chained by his wooden doghouse. Detective Ford parked the car and went inside. When she returned, she looked triumphant, and I knew I had a case. It is a shame I had to go through such lengths to defend and prove myself. I had already sustained more then I felt I should have to bear.

Detective Ford carried me back to the shelter. En route, she explained how there has to be a restraining order put into effect against my father so I could return home. Afterwards, my mother needed to take me and have me reexamined. She gave me enough details for one day. It was early afternoon when she dropped me off at the shelter. No one was there except for the counselor. All of the girls were gone to see caseworkers or attending to other business. There was not any television and it got old reading the same magazines. I decided to call Tessie. She answered the phone sounding as she normally did. When she heard me on the other end, her voice changed and she gave me the impression she did not want to talk. After five minutes of trying to coax her into a dialogue, I gave up, said my good-byes and put down the receiver. Then I tried Monica. The same scenario played out. After I hung up, I was confused and hurt by the way my friends of 11 years were treating me. I thought about the fact that I could not even call home because the counselor said my family was off limits until the restraining order came into effect.

Feeling lonely and isolated, I sat in the big rocker recliner, placing the little portable radio right at the edge of the end table. Finally, finding a feasible station, I sat there and cried. Eventually, I allowed the music to course through me. I learned to give myself over to the music surrounding me. As I lay back in that chair, the music became my escape from my hurts, disappointments and confusion. While listening to the music, I blocked out every outside stimuli, every sound, every hurt, every smell, I blocked out everything. I would close my eyes and feel the music in every fiber of my being. It would lift me and carry my spirit wherever, depending on the mood of the music. Music was my sanity so as I lay back, rocking in that chair, I experienced my feelings of total betrayal and despair slipping away with every song to which I listened.

The next day, the detective took me to Child Protective Services to see my mom. I was very nervous and as I sat down in the chair across from her, it was all I could do to keep the trimmers out of my voice.

Are you ok?

Yeah, I'm alright. I showed the detective the hotel where he's always taking me and she was able to confirm it with its personnel.

April, why didn't you tell me it was going on?

What?! I was totally flabbergasted!

I did tell you! You wouldn't believe me so I had to go out and get proof.

Well, I'm sorry about everything you've gone through, I really am. Right now, we're working on that restraining order and you should be able to come home tomorrow.

The next day, I actually went home. I do not remember if my physical was during my stay in the shelter or after I returned home. At some point, the doctors rechecked me and, yes, my hymen had been breached. I believed I had the assurance that my father would be incarcerated for what he did and I would never have to endure him ever again.

17

The day came for the hearing. It would determine if I had a legitimate case to be able to proceed with a trial. I was very nervous, but I knew I had substantial evidence. When my turn came to go up on the witness stand, the mood in the room was very somber. I was grilled about where the abuse took place, what the place looked like, and the dates when it happened. They were only able to accuse him for two specific dates, even though I was molested on well over one hundred different instances throughout my childhood. He would go to trial on only two counts of molesting me.

I was able to describe the room in the hotel to perfection. I think what sent my case over the edge and sealed it was my final comment, thrown in as an after thought.

Oh, yeah. The soap was Cashmere Bouquet.

During the time in which we waited for a trial date, I was having some problems with my knees. My mom took me to get x-rays. During the x-ray, they injected blue dye into my right knee. This enabled them to see if anything was wrong with the cartilage. When I went home, I was confined to crutches for a least a week. The dye had my entire knee swollen and it was incredibly uncomfortable to bare weight on it.

My great Aunt Vicki, my father's aunt, was visiting with us from Chicago. One day, I was laying on the couch in the living room. My brother was still in his bed. Before my mom left for work, she told us specifically, not to answer the phone. My father had been repeatedly calling, trying to snatch any opportunity to get back into the house. My brother was half-asleep when mom gave him the instructions. As anticipated, the phone rang. Tyrone answered it. A few moments later, he came bounding down the stairs, frantically blurting out that our father just called and was coming over. My aunt was trying to keep us calm when we heard him knock on the front door. When he did not get an answer, he resorted to systematically banging on the windows. He was working his way around to the back of the house. My brother dialed 911.

911. Please state the nature of your emergency.

Yes. This is 1531 Nova Ave. We have a restraining order against my dad. Right now, he's banging on all of the windows, trying to get in.

I do not know what the dispatcher said, but my brother was becoming frustrated. He finally said,

You all need to come handle this quickly before I cut him up into thirty three little pieces and I'm holding the butcher knife to prove it!

He slammed the phone down. Aunt Vicki thought quickly and had us hide in the guest bedroom closet. I grabbed my crutches and hobbled into the closet with my brother as we breathlessly listened to my father work his way around the outside of the house pounding on every window he could reach. The icy tentacles of fear gripped me. That fear escalated to a new realm when we heard my father violently burst through the back door in the basement. My Aunt Vicki greeted him at the top of the basement steps trying to console him. He said he did not want any trouble, just to get some of his clothes and personal belongings. About 10 minutes later, the police showed up. My father answered the door himself. The cops asked if there was disturbance because someone had called 911. I do not know what my father told them, but in the end, they said all right – and left.

To give us a chance to get out of the house, Aunt Vicki talked my father into going for a ride. Tyrone took that opportunity to call Aunt Sandy, my mom's good friend. I remained on the couch, numb. By this time in my life, I did not cry much. Each time my father had made advances, I would cry but it never stopped anything. Believing that tears were wasted energy, I had begun holding in my emotions. I held happiness and laughter back because my peers felt I was goofy. I was teased and tormented excessively because of my personality. I held sadness and tears back because people told me I had a lot of self-pity and used my tears to get people to feel sorry for me. The only emotion I ever displayed was anger. By the time Aunt Sandy showed up, I had a pounding headache.

Sandy took us to her house where she called my mom. We all ended up living with her for a while. In between living with Sandy and ultimately moving to Annapolis, Maryland, we briefly stayed in a rat-infested hotel near Iverson mall and also in a roach infested apartment complex in Oxon Hill. We also lived in Columbus, Maryland with another one of mom's friends. By the year of 1984, I had been transferred from school to school six different times. Even though we did not live a consistent, idealistic life during our times of transition, I experienced peace when I would lie down to sleep at night. I gained security in knowing I would not be violated during the day.

18

We moved to Annapolis in 1984. My mom had always worked at least 45 minutes away from home. She was a teacher at an elementary school there. Now that she was the sole financial carrier for our family, she recognized that this move would save her money and time. While working in Annapolis, my mom had built a friendship with one of her coworkers. Juanita Little was someone my mom could confide in as well as depend upon for emotional support. When Juanita suggested my mom should come to her church, she accepted the invitation.

At the time of our relocation, I did not have the foresight to know of the monumental positive impact our transfer would have on my life. My focus was on the disadvantages. I had built a network of friends at

Scripture. By transferring to a new church, I would have to start over. I had grown to love my congregation and I did not appreciate being ripped away from my friends, again.

The trial day arrived. Mrs. Little accompanied us as support. When we entered the court building, we waited outside of the courtroom until our case was called. Previously, I had discovered the reason behind Tessie's and Monica's severe cold shoulder towards me. I had been told that while I was *incarcerated* within the children's shelter, my father had contacted each friend and filled their heads with lies about my being a traitor and slanderer against them and their families. I did not know the extent of this infiltration until that day in court. My lawyer informed my mother that my father was using Monica as a hostile witness against me to 'prove' I was a disturbed, delusional liar. The saying is 'blood is thicker than water'. I have never experienced that sort of strong bond within my household. Something else happened that day to dissolve this belief.

When Monica walked into the hallway with her mother, I did not recognize her at first. It had been so long since I had had any contact with her. She had lost a considerable amount of weight but after faltering for only a moment, I realized who she was. Our eyes met, a slow smile growing across her face and in my heart, as she walked directly over to me and we gave each other a well needed heart felt hug. My father's attorney was disconcerted when he saw how our friendship had endured and he immediately dismissed her from the case.

They called our case number, for it was our turn

to go before the judge. After all testimonies and court procedures were over, my father was found guilty on only one count and not guilty on the other. He received two years in prison plus probation. As we left the courthouse, I had an immense, pounding headache. I knew I should have been elated about my freedom and peace for two full years, but I just could not allow myself to believe it was over. Until I was fully grown and moved out on my own and far away from my parents, I believed I would always be trapped. My past supposed victories have always turned out to be nothing more than a brief reprieve from hell, to which I inevitably had to return.

In the meantime, during that year, the relationship between my mother and I had a chance to heal and grow. My mom was a teacher; therefore, she had to find a means to supplement her income during the summer months. She chose Mary Kay Cosmetics. My mom has always been outgoing and personable. Her sales flourished as she made a quick route toward the top of her Mary Kay district. Because of her flexible schedule and availability, we were able to make Saturdays our mother/daughter day. I would accompany her to her shows, then we would eat lunch or dinner at Pizza Hut, always ordering our favorite selection, Priazzo pizza which is just a fancy way of saying pizza pie.

Juanita Little had been telling my mom about Antioch and how much the power and anointing of God was there. I did not have a mature understanding of 'anointing' or any such matters. That was not my focus, as I walked into that church. Their initial response was to welcome me with a smile and hug. I hated being touched because it literally made my skin crawl so when people hugged me, no matter how friendly their intentions were, I did not reciprocate. I did not want to be there in the first place, therefore, I found a seat as far away from my mom as possible. Soon afterwards, Mrs. Little came over and informed me of a rule the pastor had implemented. If someone were under 18 years of age, they had to sit with their parents. It was his belief that this was a working method to keep down any confusion caused by children playing. This only fueled my animosity. During that service, it was my mission to catch the eyes of as many people as possible just so I could roll mine. I wanted those people to know how much I loathed them and how emphatically I did not want to be there.

I was shocked when a meek, soft-spoken 14-year-old girl came up to me after service, warmly hugged me, told me she loved me and asked if I wanted to go to the mall with a group of young people. By her crossing my invisible line, we became very close. That bold young lady was Shanika McConney. Her family accepted me - bad attitude and all - with open arms.

19

The pastor of Antioch, Bro. Chester Wright, had an entirely different direction of preaching than what I had heard before. His messages were not focused on hell and eternal torment. Bro. Wright taught about relationship with God. He also taught about holy boldness – the ability to live above fear by having confidence in the bible as the Word of God, and His power.

At some point or another, while my father was in prison, I confided in Bro. Wright about the situation with my father. What my pastor told me was like salve on an open wound.

Yes, the Bible does teach us to obey our mother and father but what your father did was illegal and you must

remove yourself from that sort of situation. Besides,
when your father crossed that line, he acted outside
the boundaries of being a father, which negates his
privileges as your father.

I began gaining confidence and wisdom from
the only perspective that I understood; the Christian
perspective. My attending Antioch was during a point
where I questioned if there was a God. I needed to know,
beyond any doubt, what was my purpose for even being
born. Did I have a point for being here? Is there really a
God? If there is, what was his role in my life? Needing
answers only spawned more questions. Why was I so
angry all of the time? Why did I not seem to have any
self-control, even in the face of supposedly knowing
what was morally right or wrong? I gained a thirst for
reading the Bible - outside of the church setting, in my
own home, for myself. The church and the Bible were
the only ultimate *authority* that I knew of, therefore,
all of my research was Bible based. My views were
from the Christian aspect. At that time, I would have
rejected information from any other perspective other
than the Christian point of view.

Approximately one year went by before my father
was released on good behavior. A familiar scenario was
played out after he arrived home, but with and added
twist. This time, he ignored me all together. We would
sit at the dining room table for a family meal and I
would ask him a question or make a comment without
him ever acknowledging that I had even spoken. My
mother must have been experiencing some form of
pressure as well for she did something totally out of

her character. The day after my father's return, my mom had asked me to carry out a task. In the middle of my performing that particular job, she asked me to do something else. Common to most teenagers, I smacked my teeth and rolled my eyes in exasperation. My mom surprised me by smacking me in the face.

Weeks went by and I began to feel that this time might be different. My father would not speak to me, let alone touch me. Everything would be okay. My jubilance, however, was short lived. By this time, it is the year of 1986 and I had finally made it into the twelfth grade. One day, as I walked through my front door, I noticed that my mom and my brother were not there. My father quickly informed me they had gone to Missouri – without me. I was gripped by a dreadful feeling of de je vu. I experienced a brief flash back of being on *vacation*, alone, for an entire week with that man. I just could not believe, could not even fathom, that I was being subjected to the very same hell again! If I had ever felt a burning hatred for anyone in my life, it could not possibly have surpassed what I was feeling at that moment for my father and for God. God is love. God is compassionate. God is merciful. I thought, *Baloney! Hogwash! What a crock*!

I looked back throughout my life at how involved my family had always been in church. I looked at the hypocrisy my father so shamelessly bestowed, how he had always portrayed the perfect picture to the church world of the ideal Christian. My father achieved high status in church, be it deacon, minister, or evangelist. I was looked upon as the crazy child in need of psychiatric treatment. *Boy, does she have a warped imagination!*

Well, it all boiled down to one question. God, while my life was being soiled and tarnished, where were You?

My profound question would not be answered that week, nor in any of the multitudes of weeks afterward. During that week, my father made it very plane that I would die before he would ever go back to prison. I was raped during that week, tormented, threatened and even abandoned at a Chinese restaurant. I was very happy when my mom returned home.

Previously, I had confided in my Sunday school teacher about my father. She did not know about my recent week of hell. From the teachings I was receiving on holy boldness, plus my growing indifference to the consequences of exposing my father, I began to formulate a plan. I had decided within myself to tell my mom about this most recent assault. No matter what her reaction, I was not staying there any longer. For one week, I prayed for God to give me the strength and boldness to do what I felt had to be done. At the end of that week, one morning I woke up with a supernatural abundance of peace. Right then and there, I knew that I was supposed to tell my mom that day. I did not know what else was to follow or how I was supposed to do it. All I knew was that I felt an unbelievable peace and I needed to act – fast.

I must again stress that my mother and father had always pounded it into our heads to obey, obey, obey. Honor thy mother and father. Do not be disrespectful. Never say no and do not ask why. If a person has that drilled and taught to them since birth, then no matter what the situation, they will not argue or show any sign of defiance. I had to absolutely wait on God before

I could act because without that prompting, I would have most definitely lost my nerve. My father was not home and mom was at the dining room table sewing. I went into the dining room, sat in an adjacent chair and courageously made a flat, blunt statement, all the while looking my mom dead in the eye, continuously feeling that sweet peace.

Mom, he's done it again.

Done what?

He's molesting me again.

I was not prepared for her reaction.

Ha! I don't even want to hear it! I shouldn't have listened to you the first time! With you walkin' around half dressed, what do you expect? If this really happened, why haven't you ever said no or resisted him?

Mom. You know how you all raised us. Plus, what about the proof I had? Surely, you believe that!

I just don't know what or whom to believe anymore. I mean, put yourself in my shoes. I'm being bombarded by both sides and...

I did not even wait for her to finish. In the middle of her sentence, I got up from the table, and went upstairs to my room to put on some street clothes. With my mom watching in utter disbelief, I walked right out the front door. I had said to myself, *No more. I am looking out for me and I really don't give a flyin' fig about respect and obedience.* I went straight to the convenience store at the corner, picked up the payphone receiver and called my grandmother. I told her about everything. Her final words were music to my ears.

I knew that *!@ was a snake! I'm wiring you some money. You come live with me.

I told her to hold off and I would call her back before the day was over. I then went back home and informed my mom that I was moving out. She agreed that maybe it was for the best. She also felt part of the problem was the lack of confrontation and, so when my father got home we would sit down as a family and confront the problem head on. Again, I felt victorious. I thought, *"Yes! She's gonna finally ask him straight up about everything!"*

That evening, after my father had been home for a substantial amount of time, mom approached 'The Subject'.

Larry, April feels she's ready to be out on her own. She wants to move to Missouri and live with her grandmother. I guess she feels she needs a fresh start.

My father responded that it was fine with him plus, he would even put out the money for my plane ticket. Now, wait a minute! Not only did my mom not confront my dad about 'The Subject', but now my father was making it sound like I was a nuisance and he was footing the bill to eradicate a pest. Well, no matter. I got what I wanted. I was moving out!

A ticket was purchased for a flight leaving on the following night. I was PUMPED! As a courtesy, I called my Sunday school teacher on the evening before my departure, just to say goodbye. I was somewhat deflated by her reaction to my news.

April, I have a bad feeling about your moving away. I just don't believe it's the will of God.

Well, what am I supposed to do? I'm not staying in this house.

Oh, I definitely agree that you need to get out of there, but you could come stay with me just don't leave the state.

I've already made plans plus I have a ticked reserved for me. I'm going to Missouri.

Within the next 30 minutes, I received two subsequent calls - one from my pastor and one from the pastor's mother-in-law. Sis. Singletary and the pastor both believed emphatically that it just was not the will of God for me to go to Missouri. Even though I had learned quite a bit since my attendance at Antioch, I did not know what they meant by *the will of God.* I did not understand at the time that there was a Divine purpose and a plan for our lives. Sometimes, we inadvertently make plans for our own lives that could possibly lead to our own destruction or at the very least, lead us down a road that would make our lives more difficult than necessary. Also, to be perfectly honest, I did not care about what God wanted. I truly believed that if He really cared about my well being, I would NEVER have gone through what I had experienced.

The next evening, with my bags packed and hopes soaring, I boarded that plane to freedom. My moms' final words were how she sincerely wished things could have been different. With our final embrace speaking volumes, I got on the plane in Maryland on December 31, 1986. A few hours later, my cousin, Lynne, picked me up from the airport in Missouri and dropped me off at my grandmother's house. As I walked into her dining room, the irony was astounding. I caught a glimpse of her television through her bedroom door as the golden ball was being dropped in Times Square. It was January 1, 1987, twelve midnight, the very beginning of a brand new year.

20

I began to live. I felt like Alice in Wonderland. Everything was new. No one knew my past, therefore I did not have to worry about someone looking into my eyes and seeing my shame. I concentrated on what I felt was important to me which at that age was school work, my chores, and a good social life. Yep, things would be different now.

Grandma laid down the ground rules from day one.

1. Get all of your homework done as soon as you walk thru the door after school.
2. Your chores will be to clean the kitchen as soon as each meal is over and every Saturday morning, you get up and clean both bathrooms.

Besides the general rules of cleaning up behind myself, and simple common sense behavior, that was basically it. Respecting my grandmother was a given fact, one that I momentarily forgot one day. Grandma was cooking dinner. Without turning away from the stove, she gave me instructions to do something for her. I went to do as she asked. As I was leaving the kitchen thru the archway that leads into the dining room, she changed her mind and told me to rinse up a few glasses that were in the sink instead. Well, as was a customary response from me, I smacked my teeth and rolled my eyes as I headed to the sink. It only took three of four attitude laden strides to walk past my grandma and situate myself in front of the sink to her left. Seemingly, out of nowhere, she reached out and smacked me clean in the mouth, never once looking up. She never flinched, never halted from stirring in that pot. Her only response was, "You must've forgotten who you're dealing with." It never happened like that again.

My grandmother became my best friend. She was open and willing to talk about anything. I can remember one instance when I walked into the house from having a bad day at school. Grandma had asked how my day went, to which she received a 'ho-hum, whoa is me' answer. After a little while, she said, "Come on. I need to go drop this load over to the church." Yeah, grandma had her little hustle goin' on. My grandmother styled hair from her own salon in her basement. Not only did she do hair, she cleaned business offices and peoples' homes. One of her jobs that I can remember was the laundry she washed for one of the largest churches in her community. Grandma would go there, and pick up their towels and sheets, taking the load to her home to wash, dry, and fold. I fondly remember she had a specific way of folding everything. Small towels were folded differently than large ones. Fitted sheets had their own special way while flat sheets were handled more simply.

This particular day, she had already picked up the church's laundry and she decided to use that time to take it back. I went with her, quietly putting on my seatbelt in the car. In silence, I solemnly looked out the window as I watched those large stately Kirkwood homes whiz by. After dropping off the laundry, grandma and I headed towards home. En route, we stopped at the Tasty Freeze ice cream parlor. Grandma and I ordered a burger, soda, and a chocolate fudge sundae. Once we were seated and done with our burgers, happily munching away at our sundaes, she casually said, "Now, do you want to talk about it?" I so appreciated her ability to get me to open up and talk.

The school I attended was Kirkwood Senior High School. They had a great system of education. Its teachers and principals were not afraid to institute or allow new ideas and unique ways of learning. They made sure that school was fun and enjoyable. Each grade level had its own principle with one grand principle over them all. Our senior class principle was Mrs. Coco. Oh, she was great! She smiled a lot, listened when you spoke and when needed, would stop you dead in your tracks with as little as a look. Mrs. Coco aloud activities that I do not believe any other school would have dared to incorporate.

One of those allowable activities was Senior Hook Day. Traditionally, in most high schools, there would be a rumor of a date for all daring seniors to play hooky from school. Any particular date could solidify and become the student's official hook day. Well, traditionally, for all students who chose to participate, it was counted as an unexcused absence. Our school had something different. Mrs. Coco told us that public schools received money per student therefore if an entire class body were absent, the school would lose money. She gave us an amiable alternative. She told us that if each student who wanted to participate came by her office and paid one dollar, she would make their absence excused, while all others who played hooky from school on that day would get an unexcused absence. All money collected would go into our senior class activities fund.

Another fun experience was Senior Prank Day. One of my classmates told me that this was allowable as well. I was told that the previous year, someone had brought dead fish into the school and planted them in a trashcan in the library. The year that I attended, in the courtyard, someone had filled the bed of their pick up truck with sand and had dumped it in the inner court, while a couple of other seniors dawning bikinis or trunks raised a volleyball net. When the bell rang for finals to begin, simultaneously, you heard all radios come on, and the beach party began.

I lived with my grandmother for only one school semester, but it was one of the best experiences I ever had. It was the only time in my life that I had ever even came close to making the Honor Roll. I made what was called the Honorable Mention. In other words, my grades were not quite good enough for the Honor Roll but were sufficient enough to be mentioned. Not only did I excel in school, but I also excelled socially. I had a job at McDonalds, which was within walking distance from my home. I had friends that would call and invite me to after school games or activities. I think one of my most memorable and cherished experience was my first date.

A good portion of my mother's family lived within the St. Louis area. My grandmother would often go to visit my cousin, Flowerie and her daughter, Punky. On one such visit, I was on my way into the house with Flowerie's granddaughter, also named Flowerie. As we approached the door, Flowerie's neighbor pulled up on his motorcycle. Instantly, I reacted as any teenage girl would. My entire countenance changed. Time seemed to slow down, as I slowed to a lazy stroll, batting my long eyelashes. My heart decided to play hopscotch, while I breathed slow purposeful breaths. He wore a white helmet with colorful decals that caught the sun's rays on that bright afternoon. My attention deliberately came to focus on a pair of dark crystal blue eyes and a nice lean physic. After Flowerie and I were inside, I asked her about the guy next door. She said he was single and that she would see if he wanted to go out with me. Well, it turned out he did and so we made a date. I was so excited. I had never even talked to a boy on the phone, let alone dated.

The evening of my first date arrived. My grandmother was always after me about my appearance. My hair must be done at all times. She lived as she directed me to live for she was a lady of style and class. She always maintained a level of composure, adjusted to the occasion. I believe she was as thrilled as I was about my date, but she would never give the appearance of anxiously waiting for her grandbaby's date to come to the door.

Now, I'll be in the bedroom watching TV. You call me when he gets here. But don't act like I'm sittin' here waiting on you.

When the doorbell rang, my heart skipped. With much apprehension, I opened the door expecting to see my Prince Charming. I smiled. When he smiled back at me, mine slowly faltered. Never, ever assume that because a man has beautiful eyes that everything else on him will follow suit, for it is not always the case. That boy had the worst case of yuk mouth I had ever seen.

I recomposed myself, invited him inside, stepping back a few paces to call my grandmother. She responded with mock surprise.

Oh, OK.

Grandma came from around the corner as if she were not expecting any company that evening. I introduced her as they shook hands. She discretely looked him over as she asked key questions about his family and background. Once her subtle interrogation was over, she excused herself and went back to her bedroom. We then set off for our date.

We got to the mall and decided to have pizza and a movie. When he brought the pizza to the table, I took a real good look at his hands. Now ladies, we all know that a man can be as fine as the morning dew, but if their hands and teeth are not clean, well, enough said. Anyway, by the time we finished our pizza and settled into our seats at the movies, my mind was made up. I could not tell you what movie we saw, nor who was in it. All that I could think about was making sure he did not touch me and what story was I going to come up with to put a permanent cap on our evening.

On the way home, I told him I had a good time. I explained to him that we could never go out again. The reason being I was still not over a previous relationship in Maryland. I could not trust myself to see anyone else, knowing that there was a possibility I would just hurt him and end up going back to a long-distance relationship with my former love. Of course he was disappointed, and asked me numerous questions about this relationship, to which I came up with the most persuasive answers I could to further seal that evening. When we reached my home, he leaned towards me. I had expected him to try to kiss me, so I was already prepared, as I jutted out my hand between us for a parting handshake. He looked crestfallen as he leaned back into his own space and shook my hand.

I could not get out of that car fast enough. As soon as I went inside, my grandma met me in the dining room and with anticipation, said,

OK. Spill me the details.

I told her all about my evening and the nasty teeth and nails. She gave all of the 'oohs' and 'aahs' and wrinkle nosed expressions that one would expect from their best friend upon relaying a juicy story.

21

I have never really enjoyed gym class. Those feelings changed within me at Kirkwood Senior. With that particular gym class, I felt like part of a team. Kickball was one of my favorite gym games. Instead of using the standard school issued ball, we used a maroon rubber ball that was three or four sizes larger.

I will never forget one game in particular. I was the first baseman and the bases were loaded. The opposing team had two strikes against them, the school bell was about to ring for dismissal; the tension was high. My focus was on the girl about to kick the ball. The pitcher rolled the ball towards her, and she bulleted the ball in my direction. Seemingly in slow motion, by instinct, I dropped to my knees, and caught the ball with my body, my arms coming to rest around it. Simultaneously, the dismissal bell rang.

Instantly, my entire team threw up their hands and cheered me. I could have melted right where I knelt. That was the best feeling in the world. I felt exhilaration, kinship, approval, and admiration all wrapped up in that very moment. I wanted to feel that again and again, and so I excelled in everything that I did. I kept my grandma's house clean. I continued to have good grades. My job at McDonalds was secure and all of that was great, but most of all I had camaraderie.

I had been to a professional basketball game or two as a child. I was always in awe of the scope of it. To look up and around thru the eyes of a child was magnificent. It seemed like I was in a sea of people. It was wonderful to feel the cheers and excitement of thousands of people around you. I fully understand how people can get so caught up in the emotional charge from sports. It evokes the same feelings of elation and euphoria that we gain so emphatically when we are one with The Divine.

As a child, those feelings were rare for me. I bathed down to my very soul in what I felt in that arena. The crowd would cheer in unity when a player did something good. When he made a play that was great, the crowd exploded. Not only did that grab me as a child, but as a 17 year old, it affected me at my very first baseball game the same way.

A friend of mine from school, Tracy, had obtained tickets to the 1987 Opening Day Cardinal's game. I was excited, exhibiting that mellow edge that only teenagers can produce. We had excellent seats even though, now I could not tell you where they were in the stadium. Clark was Tracy's favorite player. He made an outstanding play that day, which made me feel even more special about my performance on my own team (in gym class, playing kickball that is). The final play had come. The game had gone into an 11th inning and the bases were loaded. Clark was batting. When he hit the ball over the fence and made that grand slam home run, the crowd went wild as they did when I had made my own final play. Words cannot describe how good all of that felt.

The experience of living with my grandmother was good. It was fun. I got to do so many different things. I had my first date, and went to games with friends after school. I lost fifty pounds and I felt good about myself. When I processed all of that, then looked at the inevitability of going back to Maryland, I was disheartened, even though I loved my mom and wanted to see her badly. It was the month of May, and I was already preparing myself for the customary face and the wall that I would erect between myself and my dad. I felt repulsed to even be near him. No one knew how I truly felt, because I had learned to thrust my feelings down as far as I could. I would settle into the persona that everyone expected. I learned how to feel people out that way. I would instinctively feel what other people were feeling so that I could make the necessary adjustments in my own emotions and actions to keep the peace. For the most part, I believed it was effective.

I had received an acceptance notice in the mail from Hickey Business College. I was not thrilled with the idea of going on to yet another school. I hated school and even though I enjoyed that one semester at my grandma's, I could not wait to get out. It was an expectation within my family to go on to college. I applied out of duty.

We graduated in May. College would not begin until, of all days, July 4th. Hickey, what were you thinking? Anyway, the school was in Clayton, Missouri, which was only twenty minutes from Kirkwood. I had half of May and all of June in which to do something non-school related. I really did not want to go back to Maryland, but I missed Tessie, Monica, the McConney's and the whole Antioch family. My brother had already moved out and it would be just my parents and me. Yes, that semester was fun, but it was now time to return to reality.

22

Graduation day came. What a beautiful feeling it was to walk across that stage and receive my diploma. What was even better was knowing it was over. School just represented one more thing in my life in which I was obligated to participate. I had a plane to catch in about three hours. I was going to enjoy that day, imprinting it within my memory, to call forth and savor for the rest of my life.

After the ceremony, my grandparents brought me back to their house to gather my luggage and head to the airport. After all of the hugs and kisses, I boarded the plane, took my seat, got comfortable and settled in to think. Think about what, you might ask. I had a full month and a half to fill. What would I do with my time? Would I still be abused now that I am an adult?

As I left St. Louis, even just for a month, my happy wholesome feelings were left behind, and my anxiety quickly returned.

My mom picked me up from the airport in Baltimore. For the first couple of weeks, everything seemed to be okay. As a matter of fact, for a graduation gift, my dad bought me a car. My parents had been teaching me how to drive since I was twelve. I remember after my dad had taken me to drive at the park and on the Capital Center parking lot a few times, he decided to introduce me to driving on the freeway by pulling off to the shoulder on I-95, and saying, "Drive". With my heart hammering in my chest, I blocked out the cars around me and just focused on staying in my lane and doing the speed limit. My dad had complete confidence in me. His confidence was strong enough to fuel my determination to succeed.

I loved driving. It came naturally. Both of my parents put me behind the wheel often. By my mid teens, my dad took me to get my driver's license. I past the written test and driven test on the first try. Three years later, I was the proud owner of a 1982 Ford Escort. I felt I now had an escape vehicle. When I needed to get away, I could jump in the car and ride, alone, music soaring in the wind, enraptured with the speed of my escape. Somehow, I knew that gaining the car from my dad without any strings attached was too good to be true.

Within days of receiving the car, the abuse began again. I wondered was I now paying for the car and if I was, what did that make me? Through the cloud of confusion, a rational thought came, telling me that it was bound to happen whether I had taken the car or not. I no longer dwelt on why I did not stand up to him. What difference would it have made? I came to understand that it would go a lot faster for me if I just submitted. Submission in any form became a pervading issue throughout my life.

When the date finally rolled around for me to go back to Missouri, I was so excited, I could hardly stand it. My parents were going to Chicago for vacation that Independence Day, therefore, they served as my personal escorts for two thirds of my trip. After leaving Chicago, I would be on my own. On my own...

I packed all of my luggage and supplies in my trunk. My dad taught me how to maintain my car. He taught me how to carry extra supplies for an emergency. When all that needed to be done was complete, I made some traveling music. All of my goodbyes had been said. Ready to go, I anxiously waited for morning to come.

The atmosphere was the same as vacations long ago. It was still dark and I felt six again. The cars were packed and mom had packed sandwiches, fruit, and orange juice. The difference came when I parted to get into my own car. Mom and dad rode in their Lincoln Town car, and I departed in my BMW – oh, uh, I meant Escort, for BMW was what I *felt* when I slid behind that wheel. I started the car, put it into drive, and smiling childishly, followed my parents for the last time.

The weather was not on our side for it was raining excessively. I was always a little nervous driving at night, but that day, I was good and scared driving in the dark *and* rain. My dad was in the passing lane on

I-70 and we were going around 65 mph. I felt my car fishtailing a little, so I flashed my dad to pull over. When we had safely gone across the highway, coming to a stop on the shoulder, my dad came back to my window. I explained to him about my tires, and the fact that I was scared. He then went back to his car and told my mom that he would be in the car with me. Instead of driving for me, he rode with me. Throughout my life, he had always done that. He never did anything for me if I was capable of doing it for myself. Neither one of my parents did. The speed he was going was not as doable for me as he thought it would be. Instead of taking over, he let me drive.

As we drove towards Chicago, my life replayed throughout my mind. I was thinking about all of the things my father taught me. One hard lesson was learned when I was twelve. I had been accepted into the Washington DC Children's Sympathy Orchestra. My forte was the flute. What a magnificent sound it is to hear seventy-five or more of the best instrumentalists of children, in one room, in unison. There was an instance when I called home after practice to have someone come get me. I was told to learn the bus system, which I did. Moments like that were not frequent, but often enough for my developing perspective to be affected. Dad would tell us things like:

You don't go to work somewhere just to get a check. You work to own it.

You are the best. There's nobody better than you, in anything.

The more you run your mouth, the less you hear. Close your mouth so you can learn.

Why complain? Either change it or close your mouth about it.

...And as I sat and pondered those grapes of life, I battled the growing confusion, while even then, at that very moment in the car, he was reaching, filling my mind with filth.

How can bitter and sweet water run from the same source? My mind buzzing, I willed myself to think towards St. Louis. Count the hours to Chicago. Ten. Man, it's awfully dreary outside. Rain down pouring, listening to music, but not hearing it. How quickly would I die if I spun the car out...come on Chicago! And through it all, the questions that lurked in the background were trying to strong arm their way forward. God, where are you? What's wrong with me? Am I cursed, born to suffer, then death? Why do you hate me so much?

23

Finally, Chicago. We headed to a relatives house where my parents would be staying. I hung around long enough as to not appear rude. As I headed out, I felt released, but I did not feel airborne until I was well outside of the city, onto the open highway to St. Louis, Missouri. Freedom. I had mentioned freedom before, but that experience right then felt like true freedom. I had my two crucial elements for my moments of happiness; I had my escape mechanism and my music. I thought *What more could I possibly ask for?*

Flying, surrounded by the beauty of nature, jammin' with James Ingram, Lionel Richie, Stacy Lattisaw, Luther Vandross, and Pattie Labelle, I was in heaven! I had never felt as happy as I was right then. I wanted to be in that moment forever.

Well, I thought I wanted to be there forever until three hours later when my legs began hurting. My back was hurting. I was falling asleep and ready to 'be there already' one and a half hours ago. Just how far is St. Louis from Chicago, anyway? Finally, I saw a beautiful site, the St. Louis Arch, the Gateway to the West. I was back maneuvering thru downtown traffic onto I-44 West and heading back to Kirkwood. My mind reminisced about the things I had missed. White Castles, Imo's Pizza, Kirkwood Bakery,...what? Yes, I missed my grandma and friends, and my cousin, but I was going down the highway on a natural high. I was ready to eat.

I went straight to Grandma's house, not giving into the temptations of my mind. When I got there, I quickly parked, skipping up to ring her backdoor bell. She swung the door open, threw up her hands and exclaimed, *"Oh, well look what the cat dragged in!"* We gave each other warm hugs. I was so happy to see her.

We sat at her kitchen table, each with a steaming cup of coffee and chatted about my month and a half away from her home. I slipped into the conversation a small tidbit about my car. She excitedly went outside to see it. After all of our catching up, she gave me good directions to the dorms of Hickey School, and off I went to my first true taste of independence, ironically, one day before Independence Day.

The dorms were not your traditional red brick building kind of dorms. Hickey had designated two rows of homes in a beautiful middle class neighborhood of condominiums. Our rows were one block apart, separated by a large pond. The community clubhouse was well equipped with a swimming pool, and tennis court. Each of our condos could accommodate four students.

After fully unpacking and getting settled in, I showered and changed into a comfortable pair of jeans and a t-shirt. Taking one more look around, smiling inwardly, I headed to my car and took it for a shower, as well. Earlier, when I was at Grandma's, I had called my cousin, Tracy. We made plans to hook-up that evening. Tracy had a boyfriend and we were going to a house party with my date being Tracy's boyfriend's cousin.

Finally, I drove to my cousin's house to pick her up. From there, we went straight to the party where I met my date, David. All of that – that whole party scene – was new for me. We had gone inside and danced and mingled for a little while, but it quickly got too hot and crowded. David's uncle had a van and we had all decided to go for a ride. David's uncle asked what our plans were for his van.

What do you need it for?

David replied,

The girls wanted to go to Lil' Brooklyn to get some weed.

Aw, naw. Yaw can't go by yourself. You need to have a brother or two with you. Hop in.

I thought, *Man, this is so cool. I'm doing exactly*

what I want to do because I'm grown. Who ever thought that me, April Harris, would be going to a house party, then leave in the back of some man's van, sippin' on a beer, en route to a dangerous part of the hood, to buy some weed? That evening, as an official grown-up, was the first of many wild and reckless nights to come. That night was the first of two one-night stands. When I got back to the dorm, I met my three roommates. We talked for a while and then I turned in. I was anxious to get started with school and I wanted to have a fresh start in the morning.

24

College classes went by in a blur. What I now remember most is how much self-destruction was manifested in my life in such a short period of time. What ever my friends did, wherever they went, I followed. I wanted that camaraderie from that one short semester of high school that had so uplifted my spirits. I wanted to fit in.

During each night of that first week, I experienced something new. I learned that I was one black face amongst a hand full, in a school full of white people. One often hears stereotypes about other races. I was conditioned by my peers in Maryland and by the interaction of adults around me to believe that white people were different. They got the better jobs, better schools, and better lifestyle. Seemingly natural, we think that they received this *betterness* because they are, well, better. Even though I knew the improbability of that concept (I was taught that I was the best), I was surprised when my roommates, all white, taught me how to steal, cheat, and do heavier drugs than marijuana.

By Friday, I was able to drink, or steal, and curse with the 'best' of them. My roommates and I branched out in our school and started forming tentative friendships. I got to know one person in particular. Her name was Rebecca. Becky lived in the other row of the dorms. During one of our frequent chats, I found out her roommate's boyfriend was a drug dealer. Well, now. That puts a completely new spin on things. *Boyfriend* became our personal dealer.

Not only was I supplied marijuana on a regular basis, but my roommates introduced me to another drug called rush. Rush is a liquid that came in a small three or four inch brown bottle. Teens were able to buy it in most head shops. We, as the public, know them as novelty shops of a more diverse sort. I thought it would be cool to try rush. The girls had told me it would be a quick intense high. When I inhaled the fumes, ten seconds later, I experienced an intense head rush. I felt heavy as well as heady. Drug using teens think it is comical to feel themselves being forced to the ground by a figuratively large hand. The drawback, however, was the incredible pounding headache I felt when I came down thirty seconds later. It made my worst migraine seem feeble. Also, in class, my teacher would say, "It's time for attendance check." Beginning with the first row, one by one, each student would say their name. When my turn came, my mind went blank.

I had briefly forgotten my own name. After that I never touched rush again.

25

In August, I moved in with Becky. We began smoking more marijuana and drinking more. If I was not in class, then I was either drunk or high. In the midst of trying to fit in and be 'grown up', I would go visit with my cousin, Sandra Lynn. I looked up to Sandra. She was very cool to me. Her demeanor was always so laid back. Many fellows from the neighborhood would go to Lynne's house for a boisterous game of dominoes. Competing with the cheers over the football game would be the sound of Rick James and magic 108 radio station serenading us from a radio in the kitchen.

One particular Friday night, I had gone over there. My cousin's house was actually guest free that evening. While we were cooking greens adding a little polk salad from her yard for flavor, there came a knock on the front door. Lynn went to go open the door and I heard two male voices. I peaked around the corner from the kitchen into the living room and saw a black man...along with my future husband. He was six feet three inches tall with Caribbean Sea blue eyes. When I looked at him, he returned the gaze and I was hooked.

My cousin introduced everyone, and then went on back into the kitchen, where she held our chit chat from there. Honestly, the only name I heard was that of Mr. Blue Eyes. Gary was his name. We sat side by side on Lynne's loveseat and talked and talked and talked some more. Lord knows how much time went by. Gary's friend had left sometime ago. Lynn was ready to go to bed. Instead of making us leave, her reply was,

April, just lock up when you get ready to go. I'm takin' my butt to bed.

And that she did. Gary and I sat there and talked like two old friends until close to two a.m. When I went back to my dorm, I was feeling like a love struck teenager. Well, actually, I was a love struck teenager. I had never dated, accept for that unforgettable one while living with my grandma. Before I moved in with grandma, boys were off limits. I wanted to be free from all of those restrictions and I was feeling that complete freedom for one of those rare moments in my life. The realization that I could do whatever I wanted and not have to answer to anyone was so totally liberating. Over the next few months, I definitely exercised my right to do what ever I thought I was big enough to do. Shamefully enough, I even had another one night stand. A few weeks after moving in with Becky, while lazing on the couch, I decided to give my cousin, Lynn, a call.

Hey, girl. Whatever happened to that white boy that was at your house that time?

Who, Gary? Girl, he's been asking about you.

For real?! Ooh, give him my phone number!

When Gary arrived for our date, and every subsequent day thereafter, we always ended up in bed together. That was what I figured he would expect or want. I liked Gary, but I was not going to use the word love. Love? What did I know about love? We had sex. Big deal, I thought. Yet I found myself falling in –love? Nah, let us just say I was greatly in like.

We dated for three months. As time passed at Hickey, I spent more time drinking and partying then I did studying. Once, I was even offered a joint laced with cocaine. As a result of many days and night of drugs and alcohol, and my lack of dedication to my school work, the president of Hickey wanted to kick me out, yet he gave me one more chance. If I were to miss so much as one more day of class, I was history. Well, as it turned out, extenuating circumstances would arise for me to request withdrawal from school anyway.

26

During the month of October, I noticed that my monthly visitor had not arrived. I went to the drug store and stole a home pregnancy test. Stealing had become our means of supplying ourselves with deodorant, toothpaste, make-up, or any other item we thought was small enough to be lifted out of the store, undetected. Back in the dorm, I took the test. The results were positive. After much coaxing from my roommates, we all went down to Planned Parenthood where I could receive another pregnancy test for free. It also came back positive. Now I had a few choices to make.

1. Should I stay in school?
2. Should I remain in Missouri?
3. Should I even tell Gary?

4. Should I tell my mother?

The first step was to call my grandmother. To my surprise, she did not flip. She just asked what would I do. I told her I did not know. Her final comment was that I had her support, no matter what I decided. The next hurdle was calling my mom. I was very disappointed in her reaction, for I thought we were closer than her response.

Well, what are you telling me for?

Because you're my mother . I thought it was the thing to do.

After a short pause, she asked me what were my plans. I had not given it too much thought. The only solution that I saw was to quit school and go back to my parents in Maryland. We quickly mapped out a plan to get me home. Immediately, I would have to find a job, saving up the money to move out on my own. We jointly decided that the month of April would be my deadline to move out of their house once I returned to Maryland. My car was not running, so my father wired me the money to get it fixed enabling me to make that drive back.

I had answered the questions of whether I would stay in school and in Missouri. I had called my mom. The last hurdle was staring me square in the face. Should I call Gary? Well, of course you should, April. He is the baby's father, for cry'in out loud. Even though telling

Gary should have been a priority, I quickly placed it on the back burner, busying myself with other tasks in preparation to go back to Maryland.

On October 24, 1987, I gathered all of my belongings and drove back to Maryland. En route, I had eighteen hours to play and replay the scenario from the day before. I had called Gary and asked him to come over because we had something important to talk about. By the time he arrived, I felt sick with anxiety.

We went for a walk around the pond. For the first portion of our walk, I told him about my past, the sexual abuse I sustained and how it all boiled down to feeling used and burdened by yet another man. I finished beating around the bush and finally blurted out that I was pregnant and planned on going back to Maryland.

By that time, we had completed our walk around the pond and the block. Standing in front of my dorm, Gary asked me to marry him.

Will you marry me?

Gary, I can't marry you. I'm way too young and I need to go back home.

Well, when will I get to see my kid?!

I guess never. Anyway, I've got some packing and stuff to do and I gotta go.

With that, I turned my back on him and went inside, leaving him standing there red-faced with tears welling up in his eyes, totally taken aback by the impact and finality of what I had just said. At the time, I did not understand why I treated him that way. I can remember deliberately picking him apart in my mind to the point of not only disliking him, but also being disgusted by him. I did not want anything else to do with him for the rest of my Life. Riding along, heading back towards Maryland, I felt guilty for treating him that badly. I forced the feelings down by doing a little more blaming Gary for my becoming pregnant.

I was afraid to face my parents. I felt like I had broken that most sacred of unspoken rules. Only loose women, floozies, and girls of a lower standard got pregnant, not people of my background. When I arrived at home, my mom met me at the door with a warm hug. That was very reassuring. We sat down and talked about my going out and finding a job immediately. My moving out date was my nineteenth birthday, April 6, 1988. Within a week I was working. When I was not working, I wanted to spend my weekends with my friends. My mom quickly put an end to that. She blatantly told me that I'll not be 'defiling' other people's teenage daughters. If the circumstances were reversed, she would not want someone else's pregnant teenager being a bad influence around me. I felt like I had a disease and began resenting the baby.

Time on my job progressed. I was able to put a substantial amount of money in the bank. Soon, my parents sprang on me that I had to move out by the end of January. Fine. I dealt with that. Next, my father told me I owed him, I believe the figure was around $200. I asked him for what, to which his response was he did not know but he will think of something. It just seemed like the more I tried to pave my road toward independence, the more a jack hammer was taken to that road. I felt I was being punished for getting pregnant and instead of questioning them about the choices being made for my life, I dealt with it by hating the baby even more. My suspicions of sabotage were reconfirmed when the week before Christmas, I was given just two more weeks to move out. The date had been moved up to January 1st.

I had been following the want ads in our local newspaper and found a roommate just in time. She and I negotiated a monthly rental amount and planned on my moving in on January first. When the first came, with my car fully packed, I went to her home and knocked on the door. No one answered. A neighbor heard me knocking and poked her head out of a window. She told me the lady had gone on vacation and she did not know when she would return. Well, that's just great! What was I supposed to do? I definitely was not going back home. I felt they did not want me there.

The first person that came to mind was Shanika McConney, from Antioch. I summoned up the courage to call her from a pay phone, and was genuinely surprised when her mom, Linda, welcomed me into her home. I had already confided in Shanika about the life I had lived. They understood why I was reluctant to go back. I now find it ironic that I started a new beginning on January 1, 1987 and here it was again, January 1st of yet another year, a new beginning again.

27

I did not tell my mom where I was right away. I regret that action, but I had built a self defense mechanism to shut out any source of emotional pain or possible confrontation instead of dealing with it. I had mastered that art so well until I could be in the midst of an unsavory conversation with someone, appearing to be totally engrossed in what they are saying, looking them dead in the eye, but in actuality, I was not even mentally there. I would look through them to where ever my imagination had carried me.

I finally got around to calling my parent's house. My mom did not appreciate me not staying in contact with them. She felt I had painted a picture for the McConneys of them being complete ogres. She said they would be embarrassed to even show their faces.

Again, all of the blame and guilt was placed upon my shoulders and if I were a decent human being, I would never ever voice the hurt, humiliation and torment I had been subjected to. Being made to constantly keep my mouth shut and to not express nor deal with my emotions fueled my ever growing bitterness.

One of the rules of living in the McConney household was to attend every church service. This was not a problem. I enjoyed going to church. The first service I attended with them was the Sunday morning after I had moved in. No one at Antioch, outside of the McConneys, knew of my pregnancy. I was only three months pregnant, and had not begun to show. Nevertheless, I was very ashamed and bitter about my present state. During that service, I refused to look further than my hands, which remained in my lap. My countenance was forlorn. I was bitter. Part of my anger and shame was from getting pregnant and now having to confront the church about it. Raised a Christian, there was such a stigma about sex and pregnancy out of wedlock; I knew it was only a matter of time before someone knew, then people would look at me differently.

While I lived with the McConneys, I obtained a job with a nursing home in its dietary department. I still drove the little blue Ford Escort that I had received from my father. One night, when I left the building after my shift was over, I saw my father sitting in his car, which was positioned directly in front of my car. Heart pounding, I walked over to his car and asked him what did he want. He told me to hop in, that we needed to talk.

As we rode down the road, I silently prayed that nothing bad would happen. I talked to him about my new found walk with God and anything else that I thought would keep the mood light hearted. Apparently, none of my tactics worked, for he soon pulled the car onto the parking lot of a hotel. As he parked and turned off the car, my heart was open and listening for guidance. I was supplied with the words to say and the steadiness to deliver those words.

Dad, I love you too much and respect myself too much to go in there and defile myself with you. Now, you can do what you want, but I ain't goin'.

For a moment, he just sat there and digested that bit of information. Miraculously, he then started the car and pulled away. My heart soared! On the way back to the nursing home, he told me he had been waiting to hear me say that for years and that's what freed us. Even then, ever so subtly, the blame for his molesting me was placed on me, like I held some sort of key to unlock us from this bondage. Nevertheless, I did not ponder the thought for too long. All I could think about was the fact that for the first time, I was able to stop this horrible act.

It was only after my father dropped me off at my car and when I was alone and on my way to the McConneys, did I allow myself to feel totally elated. I was accustomed to him changing his word after I had allowed my heart to feel happiness or peace. I learned not tot get excited about his declarations of 'this being the last time', because it never was.

I had grown close enough to Linda to refer to her as *mom* and after I reached her house, I told her and Shanika everything that had just taken place. I wanted them to share in my victory. I went to bed that night thanking God, believing He had heard my prayer and had spared me.

28

Six months had gone by since I had moved in with the McConneys. June was record breaking hot. When I delivered the baby, at first, I heard nothing. I saw a nurse rush the newborn across the room to a medical baby bed. Finally, I heard small cries that inflated into full-fledged wails. I was anxiously hoping for a girl, but learned the inevitable as they laid that screaming baby on my breast. Little blasts of protest skimmed my face as I looked into the face of my son.

When the day arrived for me to leave the hospital, I did not want to go. Everyone at the Holy Cross Hospital had treated me so immensely well. I knew I would be returning to a house without air conditioning and that particular day, the temperature reached a suffocating 106 degrees. I did not want to leave the comfort and pampering with which I was lavished. I knew the realization of the incredible responsibility of caring for a baby would set in as soon as I walked through the hospital doors. Virtually, I would be on my own.

I knew nothing about babies. As we left the hospital, my mom had to show me how to keep the baby's head and face covered so as not to expose him to direct sunlight. That night, the baby started crying around eight thirty. By eleven thirty, I was crying right along with him. Out of desperation, I called the hospital. I truly believed something was wrong with him. They were not much help. I even asked if I could bring him back. The answer was a resounding no. Christopher DaWann Harris finally quit crying around two thirty in the morning, but started up again at six thirty. He maintained a routing of being awake for two hours, crying the entire time, and sleeping for only forty-five minutes.

Post Partum Depression was a reality for me. I cried most of the time and slumped into a deep depression. Visions of throwing Chris out the window plagued my mind. I was afraid I would kill him. Tasha McConney was my saving grace. Each afternoon, she would take Chris and I would snatch a few hours of well-needed slumber. Even though I had the entire McConney clan to rely on, once school resumed for them in the fall, I would still be all alone with this screaming baby during the day. The seed of resentment towards that baby which I had watered frequently during my pregnancy, flourished in those first few horrible months of not being able, nor having the full desire to comfort my baby. If it were not for my godmother's insistence on my attending each and every church service, I would have lost my mind, and probably would have truly harmed Christopher. It was not the mere act of going to church. Many people attend regular church services and come away, living their lives unchanged and still in the dark about their purpose for living. I went to church fully believing in a God that could help me.

I was very accusatory and took every incident personally, automatically assuming that everyone's actions were deliberately against me. For example, there were nine of us living within the McConney household. Not only did Linda have two boys and three girls of her own, but she also had opened her doors to her nephew, Josh, and myself along with Chris. I felt that no one was allowed any freedom. That is, no one except Shanika. It seemed as though Shanika was allowed to go wherever and to do whatever she pleased. Everyone else seemed to have to abide by more rules and restrictions, even though I was a full year older than her, and Josh was a year older than me. Through eyes jaded by a bitter heart, I saw Shanika receiving much favoritism. I now realize that not only was Linda under much stress from raising five children on her own, but under the stipulations of her lease, she was placing her home in jeopardy by allowing Josh and I to live there in the first place. Also, Shanika was not just Linda's daughter, she was her confidante and steady helper with the other children. That did not matter to me at the time. Three months after Chris was born, my godmother came and informed Josh and I that a housing inspection was due and we had to move out. I gladly moved.

At four months old, Christopher finally stopped his constant crying, which seemed a blessing in itself. I had a lot of anger and resentment built up against God. I hated Him for allowing me to go thru what I had been with my father, only to replace him with another demanding male, my son. *God was supposed to be all-powerful and yet He did not use any of that power to stop the vile and degrading acts from taking place against me, nor had He prevented my pregnancy.* My whole frame of thinking was riddled with pain, anger, and confusion.

29

In October of 1988, I moved in with a sister from Antioch named Mary Branham. She was a single mother with three beautiful children. I would watch her three year old son during the day while her other two children were at school and Mary was at work. I had not had any contact with my father for a long time. I had even taken the car back to my parents' house. By discretely leaving the keys in an envelope on the seat, I felt I was affectively cutting the last tie to my father. I did not want anything in my possession that would contribute to his hold on me. I wanted to move on with my life and I could not do that unless he was out of it. Because I severed the lines of communication with my father, I inadvertently closed down contact with my mom.

Time went by and I went on with my life. I do not remember the circumstances behind it, but eventually I came into contact with my father one day. He said he wanted to take me downtown in Washington DC to maybe the symphony or ballet, and began mending our father-daughter relationship. Part of me really, *really* wanted this. Part of me did not trust him. I decided to take Chris and Daniel, the youngest Branham child, with me as insurance. When I arrived at my parents' house, my mother volunteered to watch Chris and Daniel while my father and I went out. Instantly, I hated her. I could not believe she was thrusting me into an environment with him where anything could happen.

I felt like such a coward. Why didn't I just grab the children, decline the whole evening, and go home? I still do not fully understand. Maybe I was truly naïve enough to believe that we were actually going downtown to the symphony or wherever, and that he really did want to mend our relationship. Maybe, upon that first violation when I was eight, I stopped growing up in my mind. It could have been that I was stuck in the mindset of a little girl desperately wanting a normal kinship with her daddy. Maybe I was afraid of him and I did not want to make him angry. Again, I put on my 'everything will be okay' face and my father and I headed out.

His first stop was at the liquor store. I knew I was in trouble and began to pray. When he came back out, he had to relieve himself and decided on coming around to the rear passenger side in full view of my rearview mirror. I closed my eyes and thought, *Pervert! You **will not** get your hands on me!* As we rode down the road, his words towards me became venomous.

I don't know what happened the last time but I promise you this: It won't happen again. I'm the father. You don't tell me what you will and won't do. You do as I say, whether you like it or not.

A deliberate calm washed over me. I told him that I am not going to commit sin with him and that I would not do anything with him that would defile me. When he pulled into a hotel lot, the dialogue was heated.

Either you go secure us a room or I will.

Dad, if you get out of this car, you'll be going in there by yourself. If I have to get out, I'm going directly to call the police.

Either you give it to me here in the hotel room, or I'll take it on some back road.

Well, we might as well leave, 'cause I'm not going in there.

With eyebrows up and a posture that sing-songed, 'Okay', he put the car in reverse to leave. Did I feel victorious? Absolutely not. My father was about to take me somewhere to savagely rape me, possibly killing me in the process. Well, he was dealing with a new April with a new mentality. All along, I knew that God would have to make a way for me. I could not just believe that

God would see me through. I knew He *had* to.

We pulled up at an intersection on Route 301. Let me take a moment to explain that particular section of the road. It was a four lane highway that was packed with traffic most of the time. At that particular light, there were not only cars going in both directions on the highway, but cars were turning off of 301 onto a cross street and vise versa. When we pulled up at the red light to make a left turn onto the cross street, it was as if God stopped everything. Every light in every direction was red. There was absolutely no traffic moving on this major thoroughfare. I felt that was my opportunity to jump out of the car.

My father must have sensed what was about to happen, because he tensed and put his arm across my chest. I peeked to my right and saw that the door was unlocked. I thought, "Ok. It's now or never." In one fluid motion, I unlatched my seatbelt and wrenched the door open, while my two hundred pound father tried to hold me in the car. Anger and determination etched in my face, I claimed freedom of him and the car. I stomped across the two lanes on the southbound side of Route 301 – completely traffic free – and into the Amoco gas station. I did not timidly wait my turn in line. I stormed to the window and boldly spoke to the attendant.

Call the police. My father just tried to rape me.

At first, the person just looked at me, then he hastily got on the phone. Afterwards, I called my mom.

Hello?

Mom?

When she heard the shaking in my voice, she hesitantly said,
Yes.

Dad tried to rape me.

Silence.

Where are you?

I told her the location. Quietly, she told me she was on her way. In the meantime, like a vulture waiting for the death of its dinner, my father was going back and forth, up and down Route 301, intently watching the Amoco Station. The police pulled up on the scene and took him into custody, not even one mile down the street. Shortly thereafter, my mom drove up. With eyes full of sadness and grief, she hugged me and quietly said,

I'm so sorry.

I went to the police station and, again, filled out a police statement. When it was over, I had a migraine so bad, I thought I would vomit. My mom took Daniel home and briefly updated Sis. Branham while I packed an overnight bag. My mom and I stayed together at a hotel that night.

The next day, mom took me back to my home, then went –and bailed my father out of jail. Go figure. A few days later, I received a call from their pastor (they had left Antioch while I was in college). He wanted to meet with me and my family for 'group counseling and getting it all out on the table.'

We met in his office, all three of us sitting across from him, I closest to the door with my mom to my right. My father was on her right. The pastor asked me to relay what I believed to have taken place that day. I recanted the story, verbatim, exactly as it had happened. Then my father relayed it.

She seemed to have been sinking into depression, being a single mother. I decided to take her out to get her to open up and relieve some of that stress. When we got to an intersection, she said she couldn't live anymore and tried to jump out into the traffic. She'd wanted to kill herself.

Well, Bro. Harris, how do you explain the alcohol?

It was in the car, but I don't remember drinking it.

Do you remember buying it? People buy alcohol with the intention of drinking it.

I don't know how it got in my car. I don't remember drinking it.

Then the pastor turned to me.

I believe your father suffers from split-personality

disorder. He wasn't in control and it is a clear sickness. Pressing charged won't do him any good.

I felt that it was all a set up, like they were in cahoots. The pastor offered to give me the car back 'being a single mother and needing reliable transportation' and all. I felt it was a pay off. I told them I would take the car and I had not planned to go forward with the charges any way. What would be the point? It was my word against his. If all he received was one count of child molestation when I had concrete evidence that he had taken me to that hotel on several occasions, surely he would get nothing without anything but my word.

During the whole meeting, I was very blunt and disengaged. All of that was pointless to me and I was finished with playing the quiet, meek, scared April. I was beyond frustration, beyond hope that he would ever pay for any of it. I had finally come to the realization that he would never change and I would never be around him, alone, ever again. My mom, I believed, was his enabler. I did not want to be around her either.

I began keeping a journal. I felt that if I did not write, I would explode, the emotions were so intense. Bitterness, depression, deep pain, confusion and hopelessness were hardening me. A wall, erected from betrayal and mistrust, steadily rose up to meet the baton that I held over my head. My proverbial baton represented the way I thought life should be, the way I thought people should act. Unless you were tall enough to reach it, you would hit that wall before you would ever reach me.

I kept everyone out. Love? What was that ? My

son? Oh, I cared for him. Chris was clothed, fed, clean, and – happy? People would ask why I had not gone to my parents for financial or emotional support. Please. I was not about to ask them for anything. I would have gone into a shelter for the homeless rather then allow my feelings to be hurt by them any longer. I did try to ask for help, once. Chris was not even two months old yet. We were living with the McConneys and I had not gone back to work yet. We were beyond broke. Chris did not have any more diapers. My mom had stopped by to visit. While sitting and talking with her, my façade began to crumble. Thru tears, I told her,

It's so hard. I didn't know it would be like this. He won't stop crying. I can't get anything done. I don't have any money, and I, I just don't know...

My mom, as compassionately as possible, told me she couldn't help me.

I wish that I could help you, but the only money that I have is your dad's.

Pain ripped thru me as I thought, *She's choosing him over me, again.* I did not give my mind a chance to comprehend the humility I felt adding to it the foreknowledge of rejection. Surely, my mom saw my pain. I buried it, humbling myself even more. My composure crumbled under the weight I bore. My mom gave in.

Here's ten dollars, but you can't let your dad know.

The same cycle of deception, not wanting the left hand to know what the right hand is doing, but for the first time, from my mom. I thought, *I'll never do this again. I won't get hurt by asking for anything else from my parents.*

30

While living with Mary Branham, I had grown tired of teenager-type jobs. I wanted a career. Without any occupational skills, I felt doomed to a life of working at fast food restaurants. Because of my status of poverty, I qualified for a program sponsored by the state. I began attending the Occupational Industrialization Center – O.I.C. The state gave me a small stipend per week for transportation and expenses incurred while in attendance. The employees of O.I.C became family. Mr. Gresham was the president. When I met him, I thought him to be a cantankerous relic. He was a gruff older man with glasses worn low on the bridge of his nose, always peering over them. Mrs. Wall (one of the counselors), however, stole my heart. Any kind of troubles and I could go talk to her. She would always smile, always listen, and always help. Mrs. Turner taught me how to type and use the computer. She was very sincere in wanting to teach us how to be a complete package. I did not just learn specific trade skills. I also learned how to be a lady and to express myself, giving respect and receiving it as well. Mrs. Pratt had us read for the first ten minutes or so at the beginning of her classes. I loved reading and she made her classes interesting, lively, and real. I learned that if I could read, I could learn to do anything.

In between classes, the teachers would sit and *clown* with their students. They were just like us. I grew to love them all, but there was one who I came to love and respect the most. Mr. Gresham. That man was all about taking care of business, and while I was there, I was his business. That is the way he treated all of his students. He used to tell me, all the time,

You'll never command respect until you learn to start looking people straight in the eyes when you talk to them.

Because of the wealth of knowledge I obtained thru O.I.C, I successfully gained my first career-oriented job with ITT Research Institute. There, I began as an entry-level secretary assistant, April 4, 1990, two days before my twenty first birthday. While working there, I advanced up to secretary and eventually moved on to become a graphic artist.

Living with Mary helped me mature. She was very patient with me through all of my emotional difficulties. I still, however, craved to be independent, not needing anyone else's house or help. Between the time of finding out I was pregnant in 1987, and my finally settling down in 1992, Chris and I had moved twelve times. I have lived with full families, single mothers, and friends. We have gone anywhere from having our own room, to just sleeping on someone's couch with Chris sleeping soundly on my chest. That pattern got old, fast.

I could not afford an apartment on my income alone, so in May of 1991, Tasha McConney and I got a two-bedroom apartment together. Finally, I believed I had a place that I could call my own. Tasha had her own room and Chris and I had the other. While Tasha and I lived together, another friend from Antioch, Vonnie Brooks, moved in. She was in a tight situation. I gladly opened my door to her. Soon afterward a friend of Tasha's needed a place to stay, therefore she and her baby moved in. It did not take long for me to feel smothered. Not only were there four women and two babies living in that apartment, but I was also suffocating from the weight of trying to raise a baby by myself. I look back and my heart aches for Christopher. He was a beautiful baby and yet I felt nothing towards him. Chris received very little physical love from me in exchange for angry out bursts. I would awaken almost every morning angry and feeling a very palpable weight on my shoulders. That anger would sink into depression. I always tried to push it all down because life did have to go on.

We decided to move Vonnie into my room. She had her own bed on one side of the room with my and Chris' toddler bed on the other. Late at night when we could not sleep, we would sit and talk about the things of God. I confided in her about my anger and how I just always felt so alone and overwhelmed.

Vonnie, I just don't know what to think about God. I pray from time to time and I just don't feel his presence. I feel like I'm going thru life all alone.

Girl, you need to understand that Jesus isn't on our time schedule. He is God. He knows of your needs, even emotional ones, before you ever prayed about it.

So since he knows everything, why don't I have any peace? What more does he want from me? How come I have to do what he says I'm supposed to do, you know, living righteously and all of that , but he still doesn't give me what I need?

You know what you truly need from God? You need a hug, just to remind you that he is still there for you. I know you're looking for your bills to get paid and your mind to be sound, but sometimes God leaves us in our situation because he's looking for love and to give love. If all you're praying for is your bills and your emotions and all of your needs that you can think of, well what kind of relationship is that?

Well, how do I get a hug from God? That's one of the silliest things I've ever heard of.

Hey, don't knock it until you've tried it. We can pray right now. Lord, April has been really struggling with herself and her issues. Through it all, she's lost site of what you've truly created her for. What she needs is to know that you love her and aren't just using her, Jesus. I pray that you'll give her a hug the next time she cries out to you.

The next day, when I got home from work, the house was silent. Assuming that Vonnie was in my room taking a nap, I went into the kitchen. Chris was with Quatice McConney and Tasha was not home so I had some time alone. While I stood looking out of the window in the kitchen, I was able to experience all of the same old thoughts and feelings. My shoulders, neck and head hurt all the time. As I stood there, I said to God, *Jesus, I really need a hug right about now.* Tears began to run down my cheeks, as I felt a warmth come up from behind me. It felt like someone had just walked into the kitchen and was standing behind me, praying for me. Assuming Vonnie was standing back there silently praying, I bowed my head and with my hands spread apart on the counter, I gave up. I silently cried it all out. Peace surrounded me and I did not want it to end. Afterwards, I went to my room to thank Vonnie for quietly praying with me. She was not even there, and would not be home for another hour or two. I was completely alone in the apartment. It felt as if God had given me a hug.

31

I wanted to be alone, all alone, and so one month before our lease was up, I found a one-bedroom apartment for Chris and me by ourselves. Ah, what a feeling. When I got home, no one would be there and it would be the same when I would leave each morning. That would be the first time in my life that I would be totally alone with my baby. The quiet gave me too much time to think...and feel. I felt abandoned. That is what it boiled down to, abandoned as a child by her daddy, and replaced by a monster. I felt abandoned when I thought of a God (that I had been taught) was supposed to be a God of love. I thought, *What love? I was mentally and physically forced to have sexual intercourse with my father.* I had been manipulated for so long, until I did not know whom April was. I sincerely would become what ever I thought needed to be projected at any given time. I felt repulsion at myself, and my father. I missed my daddy so much, but those feelings were choked out by the pungency of what he had done to me. If I could filter him into two completely different bodies, it would produce two different people. The one person would be full of wisdom, logic, competence, competitiveness, and direction. The other, projecting bitterness and perversity, was the one to which I became accustom.

Bitterness and hatred reigned in my life. Unfortunately, Christopher bore the brunt of it all. I hated him, emphatically. He represented everything from which I so desperately wanted to be freed. The questions in my spirit were continuous. *Why, Jesus? Why did you allow such horrible things to happen to me? How come you did not protect your little girl? How was I to know at eight years old, that You had more authority than my dad? After I did learn to call upon you, I was still left in my situation. You did not even give me peace in the midst of every storm. And I was supposed to see you as my heavenly Father? No.*

The well of bitterness continued to deepen. When money did not stretch, humbling me to ask for help, it deepened. When I went three days without eating, so that my son could have one meal each day before payday, it deepened. When I lost running water and heat in negative degree weather, or no air conditioning when it was one hundred plus degree, it deepened. When Chris would keep me awake at night with his insistent crying, it deepened. When I saw other people prosper, it deepened.

Once I moved into my own apartment, where it

was just Christopher and me, no one was around to make me go to church, therefore, I stopped going frequently. I did not see the point. I never really needed any specific excuse to not go. I just did not want to be there and most of the time, I did exactly what I wanted to do. I saw life thru eyes tainted by hurt and betrayal. It all seemed so unfair. *If God could be this great protector, how come he would not protect me? Where were you, God when I was being broken?*

32

I look back at all of the pain and even the guilt for allowing such a thing to happen to me after the age of understanding. By then - the time I knew what was being stolen from me and my body - I was already in the throws of a crippling mindset. I was manipulated. I have always been told to be an upstanding person, be the best. Embrace honesty and reject gossipers. I was *taught*, however, to expose what you want people to see, hiding your dirt. Do what your corrupt heart wants, but be discreet about it. I did not know what, or how to think. Learning from my past experiences, I knew not to go against or challenge my father in any way. I have come to understand and accept that it was not my fault.

My walk with God was incredibly inconsistent.

Sometimes, I would go to church. Other times I did not. Prayer may have crossed my mind one day, but not the next four. There were moments when I thought I was soaring in the spirit, flying, growing. Then There were more moments of depression. I had a very defeatist attitude. Anger ruled. Being in that apartment, alone with just Chris, my focus was always on him and I could hate myself now for loathing him. My eyes were closed to the point that none of it was his fault. Christopher was an innocent child caught in the middle of it all. I did not like the solitude, the quietness, nor the thoughts bombarding my mind. Three months after moving, I abruptly abandoned my apartment.

I had bought my own car in 1990. It was a '65 Ford Fairmont station wagon. When I saw that ad in the newspaper, I knew that it was a stick shift, but I only had $500, which was their asking price. When I went to the people's house to buy it, I told the woman I did not know how to drive a stick. I asked her to take me to a large parking area and I would teach myself. Her husband followed us in his own car. Once they left the car and me on the lot, I had a ball teaching me. Shanika McConney had given it her all trying to teach me how to drive a stick shift in her car and I just could not coordinate my timing with the clutch and gas. Finally, after two hours alone on the parking lot, I got it.

I went to North Carolina to visit my parents in my 'new' station wagon. I loved my mom so much. Despite the hurt and pain that I believe she had caused me, we were still somewhat close. I knew my mother loved me. I cannot understand why she let it all happen. She had to have known that my father, her husband, was molesting me.

While in North Carolina and trying to back my car into my dad's carport, I had my door ajar, so that I could look out and see where I was going behind me. Not paying any attention to where the door was going, I jammed my car door directly into the center support beam of the carport and pushed that door about 5 inches under the hood. Obviously, I would not be able to drive it back to Maryland. They let me borrow one of their cars. It was a 1987 Mercury Marques, fully loaded sedan with a simulated convertible top. What a comfortable ride on the way home.

Back in Maryland, I still faced my daily battles with money, or the lack there of. With my finances so meager, I did not always have enough gas to make it thru the week. My parents would be in town the next day. We went to church together on Sunday and on my way home, they stopped and filled my tank up. After we got back to my apartment, my dad gave me fifty dollars. I thoroughly appreciated it. I wanted to go out to dinner with them. They were going out with a couple from church, and I told them that I wanted to be a part. I thought I saw something flash briefly in their eyes between them. They declined my company. When they left, I felt the void, the emptiness, and rejection. I stopped talking to them. Actually, I sent them a very inappropriate, very disrespectful letter. The pen was my utensil of release. Unfortunately, wisdom rarely accompanied it.

A week or so later, I received a phone call on my job from my mom.

Hey, baby. Listen, we're not here to stay. We've just come to get the car. If you don't want any attachments with us, then you don't want any attachments to our car. I'm leaving your keys in the guard window down here. You're car is parked out here on the lot. You take care of yourself.

33

When I went outside at the end of my day, I saw my jalopy at the back of the lot. I could not take it anywhere because my parents used their battery to get it up to Maryland. Their battery went back home with them. With no money for a battery, and no one available to take me to my home in Baltimore that night I stayed with a friend from church overnight. I used that time, after Chris had gone to sleep, to think about what to do. It felt good to be around the noise again. After talking to a single mother from our church, she agreed to let me stay with her. I went back to Baltimore the next day and cleared out just our clothes, important papers, Chris's things and toiletries. We left everything else. I donated the car to Antioch.

While waiting for my name to move up on the

list of available homes through the housing authority, we moved around a lot. I finally secured my own two-bedroom apartment in Annapolis. Christopher needed to be settled. The year was 1991 and he would be starting preschool in the following fall. Chris would finally have his own room after living from one house to another for three years. By January of 1993, I had been in that apartment for almost two years. Angel, my friend from church, lived right behind me. She would baby sit for me, not only for my day job at IITRI, but my evening job at Rite Aid drug store. I has a great – the best – roommate. My care group leader, Lynne, was in need of a room. I was in need of not only the financial help but also the friendship.

I had peace. I was going thru a season of wanting to know more about God so bad that I would take the bus to church. Bitterness has always come along with sweet for me. The more I needed to be affirmed in Jesus, the less I liked the people of God. I could not believe that in a congregation as large as ours with so many members living in the town of Annapolis, that I would have to wrap a baby up at night and wait at the cold bus stop to get a ride to church. It sickened me when I would call fifteen or more people and no one could give me a ride. I thought, "Am I that evil, that people do not want me around them? Am I unclean, tainted by the abuse I sustained"? Again, I fell back into yearning for the one constant that I did know; my parents.

I had not seen my parents since they came and got the car in 1992, so in 1993, I had spoken to my mom on the phone and told her I wanted to go to North Carolina and see them, but I did not have a car. She told me that they would come get me that weekend. That Friday night, I had packed my and Chris' luggage. My father called and said they were on their way. Why would he call? I always talked to mom. I started feeling anxiety. When he showed up, he was alone. Curious, I asked where mom was. He said she is back at the house and ran together something about she was tired, or her foot hurt or something.

Once again, I tried to remain lively. As Christopher, myself, and my dad rode together, I talked a lot, smiled a lot and was determined that I was going to make it back home untouched. I did not feel like a twenty two year old independent career mother of a four year old child. I was ten again, trying to put up that customary front that has been me thru thirteen years of abuse.

It was two o'clock in the morning when we arrived at my parents house. My father dropped the bombshell on me when we were two and a half hours away from my house. He said my mom had to go to Missouri for an emergency with her mother. My head began to swim. *No, no, no!!* Quickly, I told myself, *Ok, Jesus, I'm your child. I royally need you right now. You cannot let anything happen to me. Let him see your light shining thru me.*

That weekend, I was there for the remainder of early Saturday morning thru Saturday night. Sunday morning was our scheduled time to leave for Maryland, not before a confrontation with my father. Saturday afternoon, Chris was taking a nap. I was feeling apprehensive. My father came out of his bedroom and called me in there. As I came in, he directed me to sit on the bed. After slowly sitting, I pushed him away from me, stood and told him, *"I will die before I let you touch me."* He responded, *"You'd better consider that child in there. This can be easy on you or hard."* I began to cry. *Jesus?! Where are You?!* I had to make a decision. Do I resist and try to flee with Chris? Do I take that chance and jeopardize, possibly, my life? Was I willing to put myself in the position to be savagely raped? Then what could happen to Chris? As guilt and shame breathed hot upon my soul, I willingly laid with him.

Do you understand what that did to me? Can you comprehend how nasty I felt? Did I give up and take the easier rode, only to wish I tried to resist? More adjectives are not enough to describe how disgusted I was, not just at my father, or me but also at God. My thoughts returned to fantasyland until my father returned us to our safe abode; home.

34

Positive thoughts did not enter my mind, often. The Divine knew that my thoughts would have to be filled with peace and wisdom to steadily pick away the mortar holding my emotional fort together. I always thought about Jesus. Often, it was not in a positive way. I would think about God and seethe. Is God good? Let me tell you what I thought God was. God was a representative of manhood, a user, the master entity, manipulating everyone and all things. I felt I had no choice in anything. Fear of God's wrath would not permit me to completely unleash my thoughts of Him. I knew God was real. The problems did not arise in my understanding of his sovereignty. My issues surrounded God's faithfulness. I did not believe he was there for me. I thought that I was created to be his slave and what a cruel master he was to me.

As I write, I have to really remain in a state of stillness and quiet for those memories to come back to me in tact. Truth has so completely transformed my heart from living in the past. It is hard for me to even conceive those thoughts now. To think that I could obtain such clarity of thought and understanding is humbling. Going back through the mist of the mind, I had to remember how I felt when Christopher was four. It seemed so hard for me to produce feelings of love for him. Daily, I battled the repulsion. Why be repulsed by my own child? Chris was a boy, representing that maleness that so disgusted me. Also, when Christopher was a newborn baby, he looked just like my father whom I felt was a pervert. My subconscious mind equated perversion with child molestation or homosexuality. Since I knew I would not molest my son, if not molestation, then homosexuality would be his plight in life. At that time, because of the religious affiliation and indoctrination, I hated the very possibility of my son being gay. I believed that lifestyle was a manifestation from a generational curse (this is what I was taught). It was believed and taught that generational curses were borne from some original sin that a parent practiced. That sin, that trait towards that sin is past down from generation to generation. Because of my belief in generational curses, and how binding they are, I thought that there was a strong possibility of my molesting Chris; therefore, I had another excuse not to bond with him. So warped was my determination in not allowing such a horrible things to happen, I inadvertently cut Chris off from receiving any physical love from his mom.

I knew Chris needed so much more than what I struggled to provide. He needed his daddy. Gary had sent me many letters, but after the first three or four, I would see the return address, and toss them. I wanted to be independent. My dad would say, from time to time, that I needed him, that I will always need him. I reprocessed that notion and brought it forth as my not needing any man, ever. I wanted my own job, my own home, and my own car in my name. Until those goals were met, no man would pass the threshold to my heart.

Well, I finally had all of the above with the purchase of my 1987 Mercury Lynx, and then as if by instinct, thoughts of Gary began to come - b*ut what did you have spiritually, April*? I had the experience of being awakened to God's spirit. There were a lot of individual experiences at Antioch, but I have learned that a spiritual experience is just what it implies. It is just a brief moment. Living from the peak of one experience to another, the valleys between were very low for me. I was in a continual state of depression and very inconsistent. I had a leg in the church with an arm, a leg, and my body outside of it, and in the midst of all of that, more and more, I began to wonder, *Should I call Gary? Lord, just send me some sort of confirmation. Give me a sign. Let me know that I am in your perfect will with this.*

My confirmation came one Sunday morning. While getting Christopher and myself ready for church, Chris came into my room and sat on the bed next to me.

Mommy, is my daddy white?

I had never shown him a picture of his dad nor had I even talked about Gary around him. Chris had absolutely no facts to call forward to tell him that his daddy was white.

Yeah, he's white. Why do you ask?

Because I had a dream last night that you and my daddy got married and he was white.

OK, God. I will take that as confirmation. The next day I called my cousin, Lynn, to get Gary's phone number. She told me she did not have it at that time, but Gary would be visiting at some point during the following week and she would get it for me. Gary had moved to Mississippi where his mother lived shortly after I left Missouri. I decided to give it a week and try back the following Monday. That next Monday, Lynn had the number and I gave Gary a call, after five years of silence.

Hello.

Hi. Is Gary there?

You're talkin' to 'em.

A short pause.

...This is April.

I could hear him thinking, whispering to himself.

April? April. Who...(expletive), baby! Where've you been?!

We talked for a good while. I brought him up to speed on Chris and his development and how I was doing. We decided he would come visit us in March. Gary made sure to get every phone number where I could be reached. He did not want the conversation to end.

I had a lot to think about for the next two months. Life was finally settling down for us. I wanted to remain single forever even though I was lonely and full of envy towards other people and their relationships and lifestyles. My desires of solitude were propelled by my determination to never be hurt again by any man. Did I really want to add a possible headache to our lives? Chris and I had gone thru so much financial and emotional hardship. I had to force myself to not be selfish and continue to shut Gary out. Think about Chris, April. Think about the fact that you cannot make him into a man. He needs his father.

March came. Finally, Gary was heading my way. My roommate, Lynne, had her sister, Starr, over that evening. I felt the more, the merrier. Gary told me he would be there around 6:30 pm or so. I got off from work a couple of hours early to get my apartment and myself in order. I had gone home and changed into stretch pants and a t-shirt. At three, I was nervous. I had affectively shut this man out of my life, hurting him in the process. How would he react to me? We had been corresponding over the last two months and repeatedly, he assured me that all of that was in the past, and he could not wait to see us.

That afternoon, I called Octavia (my neighbor and another friend from Antioch) to borrow butter. Deon, Her eight-year-old son, was supposed to be bringing it over. Forty-five minutes later, when there was a knock at my door, I thought, *My God, Deon. It's about time. I could've churned my own butter by now.* Dressed in 'cleaning the house' clothes, with my hair all over my head, I hurriedly swung the front door open, looking out at the eye level of an eight year old. All I saw was a belt buckle. Slowly, I scanned up into the face of a shadow from my past. Squinting my eyes, with uncertainty, I whispered, *Gary?* He gave me the same look. From behind me in the apartment, a four year old who had a dream, eyes wide with recognition, whispered in awe, *You're my daddy.* Gary came in and gave me a hug like he would not ever let go, then with tears in his eyes, kneeled down and hugged his son. In the background, Lynne and Starr were all teary eyed, cooing, *Awww.*

Gary stayed for one week. During that week, we reacquainted. I apologized fifty million times for leaving him the way I did in Missouri. He was very affectionate, which made me uncomfortable. If I walked into the kitchen, he would put his arms around my waist and give me a bear hug. I really did not want him hugging on me. It made me feel like panicking on the inside. I would sleep on the couch, while he occupied my bed for the week. Chris would sleep with

Lynne. Gary had mellowed and matured, but had not changed, physically. Mentally, however, he had grown to become a 27 year old with his third year on his job while owning his own home and two acres of land in Mississippi. On his third day in Maryland, Gary, Chris, and I went to Friendly's ice cream restaurant. We talked while eating sundaes. I mostly listened while Gary told me how he felt.

When I did not hear back from you for over five years, I thought all hope was gone. I didn't think I'd ever see you again. Now you're back in my life and I love you more now then back in '87. I don't want to ever lose you again.

As he took his heart-shaped gold nugget pinky ring off his hand and slipped it over my finger, he asked,

April, will you marry me?

My heart stopped. Christopher proclaimed, *I knew it!* I did not know what to say. Marriage? Did I really want to get married? *That's a long time*, I thought, *like - from now on.* Through nervous bursts of partial laughter, I responded,

Ooh, Gary. That's, um, that's a big one. I'd have to pray about that first.

That is all I would say. Gary began to nod his head.

Ok. Well, uh, after you pray and all of that, really think about it and let me know.

New thoughts flooded my mind. *Marriage is forever, girl. You had better be real sure before you say 'I do'.* I did not think about what I would gain. Refusing to give in to the instinctual response, I willed myself to think, more practically, about what I would lose. What would I be giving up to marry him? And for the next four days, I wondered and listened for the voice of God. I'll tell you what I'd lose:

- My time
- My money
- My bed
- My space
- My self

It all boiled down to not wanting to give up me. Would I be willing to give up myself and take on someone else, much less, another male? Could I compromise in allowing someone else to have a say in Chris' life, even if that person is his father? I fully understood that I had become a selfish person, so I needed to hear the voice of God telling me he wanted me to marry Gary. Our lives can be rich and full of peace if we live by the voice within our spirit and not the voice of our ego. God's voice is quiet and can only be heard in the stillness of our spirit. I told myself to listen for that Word. If I had not heard from God by the time Gary lift to go back to Mississippi, I was fully prepared to turn him down.

On the day of Gary's departure, I awoke that morning, shutting out all 'noise', so that I could hear God's response. Was I going to have to tell Gary *no* as sympathetically as possible, or was I going to be engaged towards a life of marriage? This is what I pondered while showering that morning. Out of the midst of my thought processes came,

If you stay meditative and prayerful about your marriage and the decisions made within that marriage on a daily basis, it will work.

That day, Gary's last day in Maryland, I told him yes, I would marry him. Once I had heard from God, I had peace, even in the face of my loved ones not being supportive of my decision. They felt I was marrying a man with whom I had a three-month relationship back in 1987, I had not seen him in over five years and he is only going to be here for a week. I was not worried.

Gary left the next morning. Chris and he had bonded well during that week. When his day came to leave, Chris wanted to go with him. Gary would be returning in May for the wedding, so I would have some time alone to do what I wanted to do for two and a half months. My injured spirit and emotions did not have the reality of being a mom to keep my mind busy while Chris was gone; therefore, I soothed my continual pain with alcohol and marijuana. I still attended services at Antioch, but there were parts of me that I would not allow God to touch. When that calm voice entered my mind to get up and pray, or do anything else that would feed my spirit or enrich my wellbeing, my ego —my flesh – would out-talk it, overriding it with my own words.

I don't want to go to church today.

I would much rather have those fried porkchops over there instead of this fruit salad.

I don't feel like talking to God.

I have too much to do today to go for a walk, or write in my journal, or....

Without Christopher, I had no distractions from my pain and so I tried to drown it by any means. I had never been alone. Solitude and quiet will test your loyalty to your own well being if one is used to being busy as a means of pacifying the despair in ones spirit. Women of sexual abuse suffer with feelings of guilt from what happened to them. That feeling bleeds into other areas of your life. Soon you feel guilty about almost everything that happens to you, even if the circumstances are out of your control. I felt guilty about being happy that Chris was gone. Guilt gripped me when I continued to engage in self-destructive behavior until he returned.

When Gary returned in May, he brought Chris, his mother and two of his brother's. The following Sunday, we all went to church. Gary had never been in a Pentecostal church before. When he walked into the sanctuary, his first experience mirrored my own first Pentecostal experience at Scripture church. He looked around in awe at what he felt and saw. People were openly worshipping God, with their hands raised, and tears streaming down their faces. Actually, I was a little embarrassed to have them there. Was I embarrassed at Gary and his family? Definitely not. Ultimately, I was ashamed of God. How can I expose people to a God that I truly did not believe listened to me; a God that did not answer my prayers; a tyrant. I obeyed him, even that little bit that I attempted, because of fear. Fear brought me to a place of baptism. Persistence coupled with faith brought me to a place to come to know and experience the Divine. Beyond that, fear kept me in church.

My spirit was being fed and the word of God is transforming no matter what religious affiliation, tradition, or culture it came from. It was affecting my life as much as I would allow it to, but I did not love God. Oh, I wrote about loving him when I wrote in my journal, but it was always a proclamation made in faith. I did not believe He loved me. Why would I expose other people to a God that, if it were not for fear of hell, I would not even be involved with?

God has a design, a pattern that brings full enrichment and purpose to humanity, a purpose for our lives. The Divine knew I would not be ready to marry Gary at age eighteen. Gary and I married on May 14, 1993 when I was 24 years old. It had rained a lot up to that day. Two days before my wedding day, I was riding down the street, alone, reevaluating everything, clearing my mind. Suddenly, I felt that same sweet peace. God began to speak to my mind.

*What type of weather do you want for your wedding?
Well, God, 75 degrees and sunshine would be nice...*

The morning of the fourteenth, it rained. Hard.
Oddly, for me, I did not point a finger at God. I took
another baby step and believed that he would do what
he promised. By that afternoon, the sun had come out,
and it was absolutely beautiful outside. I'm learning
that sometimes, God will allow the rain in our lives
so that we can see the sunshine in stark contrast. Two
hours after our wedding, the clouds came and it began
to rain again and rained for the rest of the day. The
next morning it was still raining when we, as a family,
departed for our new life in Mississippi. 1993 had the
worst flooding and storms I had ever seen. Because
of my little window of sunlight, I knew that God had
parted the clouds just for me.

Conclusion

It is possible to gain peace of mind after a childhood of sexual abuse. The process of obtaining that peace is different from person to person. Some women seek counseling, and that may work for them. Others seek peace through mind-altering substances, and that may work for them – for a brief time. I have tried church, drugs, alcohol, counseling, losing myself in music, emotional bonds to others, money and a plethora of other avenues. Coming to understand how my body and mind work, I have learned how to process circumstances in my life. Anything in this life that has an end, a death if you will, is temporal; just another form. By seeking peace in the midst of those things that give temporary relief from our grief, we do not learn to experience lasting peace and understanding. Perceiving this, I began to search for God. The very concept of God represented eternity for me. No changing, death or turning away from the perpetual continuity of God.

I have learned that we are imprinted by our experiences. What we experience touches us and links us to other experiences, creating a common pattern on how we respond to life in the present moment. An astounding number of women who have been molested will pursue relationships with men who do not treat them appropriately. Too many women resign themselves to relationships with men that continue the abusive cycle, be it emotionally, verbally, physically, or sexually. Those hurting ladies have not learned to live above the imprint. That imprint from the experience of sexual abuse follows them throughout life, until they learn how to live beyond it, learning how to breath, to inhale each moment afresh, unencumbered by left over feelings from the past. Life occurs right here, right now.

Awe, excitement, and dread are my constant companions, for I am standing on the brink of unchartered territory for me. Do I continue to hold on with a death grip to the religious tradition that has been passed down to me? Do I continue to walk in the fear that I will never do nor be good enough for the church, hence not good enough for God, or do I step into the void - mind, body, and spirit? I have chosen to make a paradigm shift, stepping into the void – so to speak. Letting go of the fear that comes from leaving my existing pattern of actions and thought, I experience life with eyes wide open.

My views about God, church, and Christianity

have changed greatly. What is God to me? I believe God is the master consciousness - energy, the initial spark that manifested life. That Master Consciousness has intelligent thought. Where did it come from? I don't know. I have had such profound spiritual experiences, until it would be madness for me to say there is no God. The more I probe into the mist, the more I understand my nature, the human condition, science, and the way things manifest themselves as reality. Looking back, I realize that the only times when I have experienced those deep spiritual moments have been during times of openness and focus, be it at church, in my car, or at home. I was totally present in that moment, not thinking about anything other than the present, my ear attuned to that Voice. I did not *believe* myself into those moments. *They are always occurring.* With eyes wide open, I became aware.

Healing can come to the abused,
if one is willing to let go of the pain of the past
thereby learning to enjoy the peace and
serenity of the present moment.

By living in the past, one holds onto the attributes of the situation from the past. By doing so, I had become bitter and cynical, as well as critical of other people and there thoughts and beliefs that differ from my own. Holding onto that victim mentality of *I'm being taken advantage of and there's nothing I can do about it, no matter how hard I try* is a distinct manifestation from the sexual abuse.

So how does one break that chain? We must tell

ourselves, *"I am not a perpetual victim. I can dictate how I will respond to those unsavory memories and present moments. My mind was ravaged by dwelling on those occurrences where I was believed to be a victim. The past situations are just that, the past! It does not dictate my present or my future.*

* *

We will now make a leap towards the present. These journal entries show the journey my life has taken, and where I am, presently. There will be some entries that disturb you. Your belief system may be challenged. Please do not feel threatened by the route my personal life has taken. There are so many women who are where I was when the original journal entry was written. I believe this information is relevant to many hurting women who are too afraid to express how they truly feel on so many fronts because they are fearful of the scrutiny and ostracism that may occur. It will be easy to judge me as a bad mother or calloused person while reading them. Realize that we will continue to grow as humans until death. I am allowing myself to be vulnerable to scrutiny for the sake of reaching fellow women where they are right now. As you read thru them, may you open the mind to receive. May you learn to live fully in the present moment, always listening for the quiet voice of The Divine. Sexual abuse may have happened to you during your childhood. Come to realize that you do not have to live your life today predicated upon what happened in your past.

Journal Entries

I believe we encounter certain people during our life voyage by Divine order. Gary and I ran into a lady by the name of Terry at Lowe's. I ended up going to her house yesterday for her to twist my locks. She has locks, and her daughter has locks. We talked about Reggae, church, spirituality, philosophy; everything that I feel is worth talking about. We clicked. I'll be going back every 2 wks for lock maintenance. She uses natural products and my hair feels *so* good! She told me about a lecture on May 21st at Harris Stowe College by a Dr. Menanu (?). The discussion will be about metaphysics and the African American. I may go.

Also, I found a grocery store that sells all organic foods. It's called The Whole Food Store. As soon as I'm in my apartment, alone, I'll switch to buying my groceries there. By then, I'll be a complete vegetarian, and comfortably versed in different levels of meditation.

* *

I went to take Tasha her books back. I really didn't want to draw any attention to my self and how I had been feeling about church. When she asked me, "How was church?" I told her, "Tasha, I'm coming to say goodbye to you and the entire church world. How can someone live in Pentecost for most of their life, trying to live the right way and never be changed nor their family members changed? I want something consistent with truth. If there is truly a tangible, Spirit being who was here from the beginning and has all power and intelligence, I want to *know* it and I don't think the church can fully show me how to do that." We hugged as she said I was hurting. She was so compassionate and without showing any judgment.

The next evening, Randy from Spirit and Truth called. He said he'd been missing me and wanted to make sure everything was ok. I just kind of blew him off by telling him that I'll be ok and to pray for me. I felt bad when I got off of the phone. That very reaction, that saying what I think they'll want to hear, people pleasing, that's what I'm trying to shake. I *will* be healthy, happy and one with God without fearing what people, religion, and tradition will say or do.

* *

I am on that path to being healthy and whole. Today, Gary and I went for a short bicycle ride down the bike trail. It was so incredibly beautiful today. When we hit the trail, I realized that most of it was on even ground, and some places had downward slopes, so it was fun and not too hard on my thighs. We ended up riding all the way downtown to the Arch. That's approximately 9 miles, one way. What pleasure I experienced watching the river swirling lazily, set into motion by the gentle breeze, while feeling the warm caress of the sun upon my skin. I was not truly tired until we were on our way back and had ridden to within 3 miles of home. Man, my legs got tired, my hands and arms were so sore. I was ready to get off of that bike.

Yes, it was a wonderful day spent with Gary. We are trying to enjoy as much time together – alone. Even though divorce is imminent, we will remain friends and we do love each other. I wish I could fully enjoy Chris' last weeks here before he goes off to Job Corp, but it's hard to assume that light-hearted rapport with him because he absolutely will do nothing around the house without being told, and even then, it's half done or not done at all. It has always been difficult to love (or even like) that boy, but the Almighty has given me grace and I hope my son knows that despite all of the nonsense he puts me thru, I have grown to love him deeply.

* *

As the days ware on, I feel more comfortable and willing to move into myself. This a.m., I was going to ride my bike for a few hours. To start off right, I went into the prayer room to do some stretches, and wouldn't you know it? I pulled a muscle on my right side lateral to my spine. It takes my breath away, the pain does. That's OK, though. Now that my satellite is back on, I watch more programs about traveling globally and becoming healthier. One man walked from state to state on the regular. The least I can do is walk a couple of miles, 3 times a week.

****

I have already reached my goal of 235 lbs by June 30. I weighted at work today, and I weigh 234. It's only half way thru the month. It would be nice if I reach 230 – 232 lbs by June 30. Also, I've met the goal of having the divorce papers notarized and ready to file. Chris leaves for Job Corp on Monday, and there are so many things I want to change; so many more goals to reach.

Eventually, I want to travel the world and experience all of the most beautiful, scenic natural phenomenon and environments via bicycle. God has created a splendid place to dwell. I will have those experiences.

I will be 100% healthy - body, soul, and spirit.

I will know God and understand my purpose for living.

I will be free from fear.

* *

Joyce Meyer was on. She spoke a wonderful message about walking in love, living like 'real' Christians, and that we didn't need another revival; we need a complete revolution. Her message, mixed with the last 2 days of spiritual events in my life, led me to one conclusion; Lord, you are about to put me through boot camp. At least 3 people at church told me that Spirit & Truth needs me and the talents, gifts, and message that God has given me. I give all glory to You, God, for your grace and preserving power. Yes, I've fallen. Yes, I smoked weed, cigarettes, and drank. My life is full of lies, deception, and sin, but today I understand that you are wanting to use me in an incredibly, history making way. Today I threw away the one-hitter and box. I thru away the cigarettes, I pored out the alcohol. My life I will give you, Lord. Use me. I will fast today and lower my flesh so my spirit can grow. I'm ready to allow you, God, to *change* my life; not revive it. A revolution!

* *

Tomorrow, I go to Greyhound to pick up Chris. He's coming home already on a 2 week Summer break. Lord, help me to be the type of mother that I should be for him.

I fished my hitter, & cigarettes out of the trash yesterday afternoon. How pathetic is that?! Why can't I control my flesh? Why am I so full of pride? *I want to know*

God, my spirit cries out all the time, but my flesh is so strong. Break me, Lord. Prove your power to me. You talk to me all the time in your own subtle ways, but Lord, I need an Earth-shaking transformation. Help me.

* *

So many changes, yet so much stays the same. Gary had back surgery this past weekend. Because he is now house ridden for the next 2 weeks, my mom came to stay for that whole time. Also, my cousin, Lynn, is living with us until we move. We filed bankruptcy and we are going to be moving into a small apartment. Gary's niece, Maria, and her boyfriend, Ureal, is also staying with us. I have a full house, which is running very smoothly, to my surprise.

Those are the changes. Here's what stayed the same. I'm still in school and doing well. I'll make the Dean's List again this quarter, making it 2 quarters on the list - 1 quarter on the Dean's Honor Roll, and one quarter with a B average. I start clinicals next Tuesday. I'm excited and quite nervous at the same time. I still work at Gateway Medical Research, but only part-time.

Spiritually, I'm so ready to go away. I want a sabbatical. I need to go where it's me, God, and my natural surroundings, totally stripped of TV, media, people, influences, and distractions. That's what life seems to be right now; just one big distraction from what's important. I want to be complete, healthy, not looking for humanities approval or love. That's why I can't let go of the weed, cigarettes, harsh music, drinking, cussing, living a life of death. That's what it all boils down to: *Life and Death*. To be complete is to be one with God. God is *life*.

* *

I finally did it! I've broken free! Right now, I'm sitting on my mom's bed in Jackson, MS. Over the last month or so, ever since I started clinicals for school, and Maria, Ureal, & Lynn moved in, and Gary had his back surgery, life has been overwhelming for me. I'm getting divorced. Yesterday, he drank all day long. I told him at 5:30 that if he took another drink, I was leaving. Either he didn't take me seriously, or he didn't care, so when he made that final drink, and left the house, I packed as much of my belongings as I could and I left. I called Chris at Job Corp and made him aware with as much softness as I could, then I called his dorm and told the authority figure to set him up with someone to talk to so he doesn't have a melt down. Now I'll sit here today, while my mom's at church and make my to-do list. I'll probably go back to MO on Thursday to get the rest of my stuff and handle final affaires with the bankruptcy and school – and work. Life's going on.

I have mixed emotions. I am either crying or just dazed. This is a big adjustment. I've been with Gary for going on 13 years. Now that the tie is severed, it will take time for me to grieve the death of our marriage. Once I'm healed, whole, and established here, the happiness will come.

* *

My mom and I just got back about an hour ago from getting almost all of the rest of my things. We were able to pack everything into the car accept my grandmother's lamps and boxed-up stuff, my book lamp, shoe rack and a couple of boxes of books. I feel so liberated as I sit here on my pallet in *my* room in my moms apartment, yet I have to fight off guilt and condemnation because I know Gary is hurting right now. He loves me so much, but I just cannot live with the cursing, drinking, vulgarity, sex, comments, lewd jokes, unwillingness to grow spiritually, irresponsibility with money, and disregard for my personal quiet time.

* *

I am content. I'm sitting here, undisturbed and writing. How much better can it get? Well, I could be employed and in school, but that will come. I've put out 12 applications and I have an appointment with the dean at Hinds Community College on Tuesday. I hope that they will go ahead and place me in the Surgical Technologist class at their school.

Tessie, Monica, and I have rekindled our ties. While I still talked to Tessie from time to time, I hadn't talked to Monica in almost 15 years. We talked for quiet a while this evening.

My brother, Ty, is doing well in Dallas, TX. He has his own website where he can give spiritual and practical advice. I'm glad he's in my life. We were talking about names and the importance behind them within each culture. I told him of my experience in my mom's living room. It was 2 a.m. or so and I was meditating on God. Seemingly, out of the blue, just as clear as if someone were in the room speaking it, the name *Wapani* sounded in my head. I had never heard it before so today, I went to the library to look it up on the internet and to my surprise, it was there, spelled exactly as it was given to me. It's a Navajo verb. It means 'the give away'. More specifically, it means the giving away of something valuable without expecting anything in return. My name will be Wapani Asantewah Savage.

* *

Greetings & Blessings to myself from myself, Wapani. Life is settling into what it should be for me. No, I'm not working, yet. Yesterday was Thanksgiving and all job prospects claim that it will be next week before I hear from anyone. That's fine. I'm continuing to learn how to be patient. At Hinds College, Dean Mahaffey said I'll start in January of '06 to continue my Surg. Tech. degree and will still graduate this summer (yeah!).

All I have to worry about is financial aid. Because we filed bankruptcy, I know I won't get a loan unless by the grace of God. I desire a job with a hospital that will pay for my education. That will be my mantra until it comes to pass.

In the meantime, I'm trying to settle into myself. I have peace. I walk every a.m. around sunrise: 3 miles. I've lost 6 pounds in 3 weeks (or since November 5th). I'm wearing my locks straight and have disciplined myself to tie them down every night. If I find the cultural scene around here, all will be beautiful in the world.

* *

I've secured a job as a phlebotomist at St. Dominick Hospital in Jackson, MS. It's only 2 exits up 55 S from my mom's home. It pays $9.15 an hour, but the benefits are wonderful, and they'll pay for me to go back to school to get my RN degree. I guess I'll be living in MS and with my mom a few years longer than I thought. She's been a true blessing and we get along pretty good.

I'm still caught in my lifelong dilemma of spirituality. God,...I know He's there, a true spiritual being, but the church is an impotent shell trying to represent an all powerful God. If I weren't staying with my mom, I wouldn't even go to church.

I just want to be happy, whole. I'm tired of guilt and smothering sobriety in always thinking about how my actions or thoughts are affecting everyone else while I'm stifled into nothingness. I truly feel that if I lived alone, I wouldn't have these struggles within myself. A sabbatical is really what I desire. I want to save enough money to go to Brazil for 1 year. I want to leave this place of stress and spiritual influences. I desire to leave, having paid all debts and my affairs all in order so that when I go, nothing will be weighing me down. I want to be done with nursing school (St. Dominick won't pay for Surg. Tech., so I'll go after RN instead), have a job waiting for me in Brazil, then travel with about $25,000 available to me. I'll work, and ride my bike, explore nature, take tai chi, learn from Zen masters about spiritual control and understanding. I want to be one with God, distraction free. That's all I've ever prayed for. In essence, I want God and I want him to want me back.

* *

My God has blessed me with a better job. American Medical Response – AMR – Ambulance Service called and offered me a position as a dispatcher. It's even better than St. D's; $13.55 per hour. They'll pay for EMT, Paramedic, and RN school. After training (3 months), I'll get a .90 per hour raise, plus I get a $3,000 sign on bonus. If I work on the weekends that I'm supposed to be off, I get a $100 per day stipend.

I don't think I'll stay with mom for too long. Even thought she doesn't come right out and say that she feels I'm carnal or backslidden, I think she drops hints in her demeanor and conversation. I plan on moving into my very own place by my birthday. I'm still very grateful for my brother Ty and our relationship. I know that he's used of God and full of wisdom and spiritual understanding and I know his level of liberty comes from not living under someone else's expectations or roof. That's what I want, yearn, need, and will have.

* *

I can no longer gauge my life by some 4th century Europeans concept of right and wrong. My God, creator of all things, in all things, all spirit, all knowing of the entire universe, is *huge;* infinite. The very concept of the Divine escapes our frail, finite minds. How boldly ignorant, if not arrogant to even fathom that we can contain all we need to know about him in one tiny collection of 66 books. The creation story and the flood story; I've read in other scripts dating thousands of years prior to the construction of the bible with completely different characters but because some 4th century European counsel says that they feel certain books are from God therefore that makes it so? Never. I denounce that theology and its dogma and restrictive practices. My God is turning everything my hand touches into gold right now. Why? Because I'm on the right path of enlightenment. My God, I will follow you and not man. What liberty in even declaring it. I will live as the Divine says live and the Spirits' light will shine thru me brighter than what I've been programmed to think could be possible.

* *

What is life but for the living? When we learn to embrace life, exude life, live it, breath it, taste, touch... *be life*, we will then exhibit life and we will be like God, reflecting that Divine image.

* *

African, Asian, and Native American art will be throughout my home. Quiet, soothing music, an environment conducive to meditation, spirituality, and deep probing conversation. I can't wait. I'll be able to walk thru my home naked if I desire. I'll build an extensive library on spirituality, focus, Buddhism, Native American beliefs, just a broad reference about the supernatural as well as natural things. Eventually, after education, weight loss and physical training, I'll travel the globe, bicycling thru beautiful mountains, near babbling brooks, living life without reservation nor condemnation.

* *

I am realizing that this job, this present living environment, life's pressures, everything I experience from one day to the next, is all an illusion. One day, I will be able to travel, to live in Brazil, to go on frequent sabbaticals. I don't want to feel the companion of anxiety any longer. Anxiety about my job, performances, and how I'm perceived by others. Anxiety over how I drive and how it affects others on the road (petty things like driving 40 mph vs. 43 for the convenience of the ones behind me), anxiety about my son and his affairs and well being, anxiety about my soon to be ex-husband and how my decision for a break up has affected his life. Throughout my life, I've always had goals, wrote them down, then tried to follow a path to the conclusion, but lack of continual focus always has me falling off the bandwagon. I'd like to find a Buddhist monk and study focus, leaving anxiety, living in the now, and freeing myself, spiritually. Was there a Jesus? I believe so. Was he *The Deity*? I just don't know about that one. I've followed the Christian path and it led me nowhere, but frustrated and unchanged. If I gain focus and direct connection with God, I think I'll be OK.

* *

So much is changing; *everything* is changing in my life. My spiritual views have drastically changed. Do I believe Jesus died for the sins of mankind? I believe that God robed himself in flesh several times throughout mankind. Buddha, Shri Krishna, Jesus, all came in their time, in the appropriate era for humans to have a focal point, an example.

* *

What is that thing that snatches my desire to write, to catalog my feelings? Is it fear? I've learned that an addiction is the manifestation of one's fear to change. Why do we hold on (with a death grip) to unhealthy, unwholesome 'traditions' – the tradition of physically placing toxins and death into our bodies and psychologically placing poison into our spirit, all under the guise of tradition? I am beginning to discern why I won't meditate, center myself, or communicate with God, daily. Fear and addiction. Most humans are addicted to drama, to crises, because that's what we know, what we are accustom to. It's hard to leave our comfort zones and step into change; at least I know it's hard for me. Who am I? I am healthy. I think thoughts that bring me life. I eat food that sustain life. I listen to music that brings life to my spirit. I'm ready for change; a change into wisdom, understanding, and action.

* *

This morning, I awoke, meditated and changed. I am healthy, embracing life, embracing God today. No fear of opinion, no fear of rejection from people, my mind interpreting that rejection as ultimately from God. I am walking in the now and the 2nd doctrine of the perennial philosophy which states that we have a divine intuition; God can speak directly to my spirit whatever needs to be there. Speak to me Lord. Give me an ear to hear and will to obey.

I was grossed out by the very concept of eating turkey a couple of days ago. The texture reminded me of the cadaver lab when I was in Surg. Tech. school. It was the same gray, stringy, lifeless meat; and we eat death every day. No more. No chicken, fish, turkey, anything that had a momma. For how can putting death into my body bring forth life?

* *

Ben, from B shift nights at AMR is like a kindred spirit. He's into philosophy, mysticism always reading and searching for the truth about our existence. We are on the same path. He was raised devout Pentecostal and reached a point where he did not believe it as it was taught to him any longer. His life/thinking so totally rings a bell with my own. Is there a Satan/devil out there trying to deceive me? I don't know anymore. What I do know is I have had some very real supernatural experiences in the church. My question is, was I feeling the experiences because of the doctrine that I believed in or is it faith in God and being surrounded by like-faithed people and because of that unity of spirit, God visited us? The whole time I was in church, from age 11 to age 36, I've called out to God for a distinct change in my life. I've wanted to feel connected and to change/dismiss those elements in me that would separate me from God, but for the most part, I've been met with a sense of distance from God and I still do the destructive things to myself that I've been doing. I've read the entire bible several times. I've studied passages of scripture, tried to retain it's info, commit it to memory and pattern my life around what I've read, to no avail. I've never been able to be obedient to it, to change my actions hence change myself for the better. I've seen people so caught up in the doctrine but because of the – what I perceive to be -separatist attitude (*if you don't belong to my congregation, doing what I do, I won't associate with you-* mentality), their pride reeks to me. We talked about other people while trying to appear as thought we're not. We talked about carnal nonsense (be it at home, before church service, during offering, or even alter call, and after the service was over), but swore we are the elite of the Christian society because

we were Pentecostal; we had *the truth*. My God! I don't
want to live like that nor associate with people who are
like that anymore.

I've had my experiences in God because I search after
Him/Her. No Jesus, Buddha, Mahdi, Krishna, nor
Mohammad can save me. I know there is a God, creator
of all things because I've had very real, concrete
supernatural experiences where we've connected. If
there is a Satan and demons trying to trip me up in my
quest while I'm searching for God, I'd think God would
cover/enlighten/protect me and that the God power is
eminently more powerful than Satan power.

* *

I don't think I write enough, so I'll try to write more
often. Maybe, then my thoughts won't be so scrambled
all the time. I still battle fear. So much is happening
in our world today. Israel has definitely become the
hot spot. Suicide bombs, death threats, their hatred
of America, all seem prevalent right now. The bible
speaks in prophecy of the pale horse in the book of
revelation but that isn't necessarily true. That Greek
word interpreted as pale, also interprets as green.
Green is the national color of Iraq where so much death
is occurring.

God, again, I cry out to you. Heal my faith in you.
Take me back to when I was a little girl and heal me.
Help me to see you thru untainted eyes. Traditionally,
that's the way I've been praying for al least 20 years,

to no avail. I must believe and do something different, for if you do the same old thing, I'll get the same old results.

* *

I went to church today. Mom said a particular evangelist was preaching a revival starting today. I remembered him from Antioch days. He'd come to evangelize and God would meet us in that place. I went to church with much anticipation. Come to find out, it was the grandson that would be at church today. I found a seat near the back. The service was the same as any other I'd attended. The pastor waves his hand in a certain gesture and the people crescendo in their clapping. *Stand up, sit down, say amen, turn to your neighbor and say....* It's just all so choreographed. When the evangelist stood to speak, after watching him for a few minutes, he began to remind me of so many popular TV evangelist. The form became fact when he dramatically made a large step across the platform as though stepping precariously from one foundation into a fully separate place, and said, "It's time to walk into your destiny!" The antics, the same words, gestures, and response. The same old actions, resulting in the same old results. No change, nor power in peoples lives. It was all very typical of what I've always seen in church, yet people don't have a clue of the realness, power, and purpose of God.

* *

I always have the fondest notions, thoughts of grandeur, of what I should, could or would do, but those thoughts are never provoked into actions. Like a caged animal, with the door left ajar, I just stood in the cage, not venturing out of confinement. My mind, my focus is scattered. I find myself flirting with depression and insecurities all the time. I have no reason to be depressed. I'm finally alone in my own place. My rent is paid. I'm healthy, have food, clothes, and shelter. Walk in the now, Wapani. It's OK to be happy right now! Stop making everyone else's drama an issue for you. Be content with *you*, even when others are not happy with you or themselves.

* *

I have been through horrific pain; pain of molestation and rape, betrayal, rejection and self-loathing. In the aftermath of all that has happened to me, **I am still here**. What can humanity do to me? Coworkers cannot hurt me anywhere near what I've already sustained. People in various levels of relationships with me will never be able to put me through what I've already experienced.

Wapani, it's you and the Divine. Get that in your spirit, girl. Don't put your emotional energy into people; not right now. All of the time spent, emotional, and brain space used in anxiety over people and what they think of you, put that into meditation on the Divine. You'll reap greater benefits. What is this life, but a fleeting moment? Why trip on people and their responses toward me? When I determine within myself to grow, spiritually, balancing myself – body, mind, and spirit – then everything else falls into place. I must see, know, and understand God and nothing or no one else matters until I secure within my own mind who I am and why I am here.

* *

I'm learning that everything is in the mind. Perspective, belief systems, all things experienced in life are contingent upon what's going on in the mind. What do I think? What have I determined to be reality for me?

I am a queen, heir of the Divine. I care for my body, open to life's experiences. I'm not worried about what others think or do concerning me. I don't smoke anymore because I no longer need to for the validation of my *grown-up-ship*. I don't need to fit in. I am complete.

* *

Today, I stepped further into presence. I had fallen ill, losing time off work. Money is bad right now. Instead of my customary anxiety and worry over what I cannot fix, I released it, and told myself,

I cannot produce money that I don't have. I am handling my money better now than at any other point in my life. If I lose everything, so be it. I am at peace in my situation.

My countenance did not change. My thoughts were not

consumed with dread and doom. I maintained my level of peace even within the midst of my storm. That is a dramatic difference from how I would have previously handled the problem. I normally will stress about most things, even things that take place only in my head. I usually have a mind full of clutter, my imagination fabricating scenarios that could have happened within any given situation. Now, I meditate on a daily basis. I have learned how to say *no* to a lot more things that could potentially bring me death. I have not arrived, but I am well on my way. I finally have peace.

* *

The image is dying and only I will remain. Such a sweet death comes to what April thought people wanted to see, hence my constant defining an image by what others think of me. No more partaking in what I subconsciously think will make me fit in with others. Freedom is here. My former hurts, disappointments, abuse, and confusion cannot affect me as I live in this present moment. Wapani, you are living, and there are many things you must master, but one thing is for sure: I press towards the mark that is the untainted representation of our Divine nature. I will reflect God, and God in me.

* *

Resources

RAINN – Rape, Abuse, and Incest National Network (www.rainn.org)

SARA – The Sexual Assault Resource Agency (www. sexualassaultresources.org)

Free Support Groups – (www.freewebs.com)

Sexual Assault Support Services : SASS – (www. sassanh.org)

Safe Horizon: Rape and Sexual Assault – (www. safehorizon.org)